THIS, THAT AND THE THIRD

THIS, THAT AND THE THIRD

The Shaniya Davis Kidnap, Rape and Murder:
The Space Between Monster and Saint

Abigail Hickman

Grateful Steps
Asheville, North Carolina

Grateful Steps Foundation
333A Merrimon Avenue
Asheville, North Carolina 28801

Copyright © 2016 by Abigail Hickman

Library of Congress Control Number 2016907672
Hickman, Abigail
This, That and the Third
The Shaniya Davis Kidnap, Rape and Murder:
The Space Between Monster and Saint

All Biblical citations herein are to the THE HOLY BIBLE, NEW
INTERNATIONAL VERSION® NIV®
Copyright © 1973, 1978, 1984 by International Bible Society®
Used by permission. All rights reserved worldwide.

Lyrics on page 233 from *Road Rash Jailbreak*
are included with permission granted by The Mad Caddies.

Cover photographs by Simeon Hickman
Additional photographs are as credited.

This is a true story. Some names have been changed
to protect the privacy of the individual.

ISBN: 978-0-9962490-8-9 Paperback

Printed in the United States of America
Lightning Source

FIRST EDITION

All rights reserved. No part of this book
may be reproduced in any manner whatsoever
without written permission from the author.

www.gratefulsteps.org

For my children, Alexandra, Andreana and Jacoby
Dedicated to my husband, Simeon Martin Hickman

CONTENTS

Cast of Characters	xii
List of Convictions	xiii
Author's Note	xiv
The 911 Call	xv

GODDAMN CEMETERY	1
FRAUD	11
CHOCOLATE MILK	14
VOYEURISM	18
MURDERPEDIA	22
MARIO ANDRETTI	29
IN THE BEGINNING	31
PYTHAGOREAN THEOREM	33
ALPHA DOG	36
TITANIC	41
APPROPRIATION	49
THE DSS DEBACLE	57
PIZZA	62
SHARK	68
GETTING OFF	75
AND SO IT BEGINS	77
HEROIN AND OTHER ADDICTIONS OF MINISTRY	79
HUNTING	86

BEGGAR, BEGGAR	91
TWO BIG DOGS AND TWO LITTLE CHILDREN	99
THIRTY-EIGHT MINUTES	101
SUBURBAN SANCTUARY	104
BROWN	111
DIRT	114
FIVE FRAIL STEPS	120
HIDDEN	122
THE BLUE BLANKET	126
MUFFIN	133
ASPHYXIATION	139
LAMB TO THE SLAUGHTER	145
THOUSANDS OF BONES	156
THE HUMAN CONDITION	159
A MIGHTY FORTRESS	163
SENTENCING	170
SANITATION	172
THE DUNCE CAP	175
BTU	185
DIVORCING GOD	193
WE HAVE A SITUATION HERE	200
AGITATED AND PRESSED	209
MIRROR, MIRROR	218
FLASHLIGHT	221
COLLECTIVE CONSEQUENCES	228
BRENDA DAVIS	228
MARIO MCNEILL	232
TURNING HIMSELF IN	232

POLICE INTERROGATION	234
PROBLEMS IN COURT	237
PSYCHOLOGICAL EVALUATION	239
SENTENCING	240
ANTOINETTE DAVIS	243
RED CHAIR, YELLOW CHAIR	254

Appendices
  Appendix A: McNeill's Letters from Prison   267
  Appendix B: Transcript of Davis' 911 call   268

On Tuesday, November 10, 2009, 5-year-old Shaniya Davis was taken from her home in Fayetteville, North Carolina, at 5:27 in the morning. She was driven about thirty miles away and raped inside room 201 at the Comfort Inn in Sanford, North Carolina. Shaniya was then murdered by asphyxiation and her body dumped into a kudzu-thick area off Highway 87 that links the two towns. She was discovered six days later after an unusually cold and rainy week. Her mother, Antoinette Davis, was accused of selling Shaniya to cover a $200 drug debt to family friend Mario McNeill who was charged with her rape and murder.

"The State never had evidence of any debt that Davis owed McNeill money. The statements that the debt was for drugs were false," Billy West, Cumberland County District Attorney—statement made to the press after the sentencing of Antoinette Davis, Friday, October 18, 2013.

Antoinette Davis photo credit: www.WRAL.com

Cast of Characters

Shaniya Davis: Five-year-old girl who was kidnapped, raped and murdered. Daughter of Antoinette Davis and Brad Lockhart.

Antoinette Davis: Mother of Shaniya Davis convicted of selling her daughter to cover a $200 drug debt.

Carlesio Davis: Antoinette's firstborn son. He was seven years old the night Shaniya was kidnapped.

Brenda Davis: Shaniya's aunt, Antoinette's sister.

JeRoy Smith: Brenda Davis' live-in boyfriend.

Priscilla Ann Summers: Antoinette and Brenda's mother. Shaniya's grandmother.

Clarence Coe: Antoinette's boyfriend and father of the child she was pregnant with the night of Shaniya's kidnapping.

Brad Lockhart: Shaniya Davis' biological father, Antoinette's employer.

Vickie Sue Coleman: Brad Lockhart's first wife who was murdered along with her little sister, Chantel, shortly after her divorce from Lockhart.

Mario McNeill: Local drug dealer convicted of the kidnap, rape and murder of Shaniya Davis. Drug friends with JeRoy and Brenda Davis.

The Honorable Judge Ammons: Presiding judge in both McNeill and Davis trials.

Billy West: Cumberland County District Attorney, prosecuting attorney for both Mario McNeill and Antoinette Davis.

List of Convictions:

Antoinette Davis (1177095) Sentence: for 17 Years 6 Months to 21 Years 9 Months

Rape of Child by Adult (Conspiracy)
Kidnapping 1st Degree of a Minor (Principal)
Human Traffic of a Minor
Child Abuse – Prostitution (Principal)
Murder Second Degree (Principal)
Sexual Servitude Minor (Principal)
Indecent Liberty w/Child (Principal)
Child Abuse Sexual Act (Principal)

Mario McNeill (0788387) Sentence: Death

Sexual Offense with Child by Adult (Principal)
Kidnapping 1st Degree of a Minor (Principal)
Human Traffic Minor
Child Abuse – Prostitution (Principal)
Murder First Degree (Principal)
Sexual Servitude Minor (Principal)
Indecent Liberty w/Child (Principal)
Child Abuse Sexual Act (Principal)

– North Carolina Department of Corrections
www.ncdps.gov

Author's Note

I entered the research for this book with a strong belief that Antoinette Davis was guilty of the crimes which put her in prison for twenty-one years and nine months. While the crimes themselves were complex, the evidence pointed to a simple explanation. Although there was scant forensic evidence, there were video tapes, eyewitnesses and a paperwork trail. Additionally, Antoinette actually confessed to selling her 5-year-old little girl to Mario McNeill who raped and murdered her within two hours of the transaction. The crime, then later the sentencing, appeared very straightforward.

But every placid lake has a murky bottom and as I dove deeper and submerged longer, I came to doubt the surface explanation of the events. Under Shaniya Davis' body lay a confusing and disturbing story. Antoinette may hold guilt, but I have come to believe that she is not guilty of her convicted crimes but rather of something more common and therefore more alarming. She is guilty of fear. It is a crime common among humanity.

The 911 Call

It was November 10, 2009, at 6:52 in the morning when Antoinette Davis called 911. It is a weighted irony that *Sesame Street*, a show designed for children Shaniya's age, made its debut on a November 10 forty years earlier. That morning the producers ran a special episode to mark the event called *A Celebration of Life on the Street*. Later, that title would mark something much more menacing in that both Shaniya's mother and her killer had indeed lived rough lives on the street. But on this morning, in 2009, Shaniya was decidedly not watching *Sesame Street* but was, instead, living the last hour of her life as a passenger in a borrowed, black Mitsubishi Galant driven by Mario McNeill, an accomplished pedophile. It was to be a gruesome final hour. But at this moment, just before seven in the morning, there was fear, yes, but there was not yet despair.

> OPERATOR: *911 what is your emergency?*
> CALLER: *Yes, ma'am. My name is Antoinette Davis at 1116A Sleepy Hollow.*
> OPERATOR: *Okay, okay, ma'am, how can I help you?*
> CALLER: *I woke up this morning and my daughter was not in the house. I don't know if she walked out, or I don't know what's going on, but she's not here.*
> OPERATOR: *How old is your daughter?*
> CALLER: *She is five . . .*

> I hope to hell when I do die somebody has sense enough to just dump me in the river or something. Anything except sticking me in a goddam cemetery. People coming and putting a bunch of flowers on your stomach on Sunday, and all that crap. Who wants flowers when you're dead? Nobody.
> – J.D. Salinger, *The Catcher in the Rye*

Goddamn Cemetery

ONCE DR. THOMAS Clark, Deputy Chief Medical Examiner, finished with her body, little Shaniya Davis was moved to the Manna Church on Cliffdale Road in Fayetteville, North Carolina, for her very public memorial. Sometime between her short but grim visit to the coroner and her arrival at the church, Nancy Grace, who reported on this case with her characteristic revulsion at the criminal while simultaneously capitalizing on the crime, stirred a particularly famous viewer into an emotional froth of action. Former National Basketball Association star Shaquille O'Neal watched the Nancy Grace episode that detailed the autopsy report and became so moved by the broadcast that he asked for, and received, the honor of paying for Shaniya's funeral and burial. His office stated that he felt compelled to pay for the funeral, saying, "What happened to her was tragic. I wanted her to have a funeral that would be as beautiful as she was." His sentiments, while generous, are not unusual. Humans feel a true sense of helplessness at such a loss. Death is no respecter of taxonomies, and while those with larger bank accounts may have the resources to delay death, it will come for all of us when and how it wishes.

And once it does, those who remain among the living busy themselves with the industry of the funeral and burial either as a way to maintain focus away from the hollowed-out spot their person once filled, or, for those lucky enough to believe in an afterlife, as a preparation for the next world. This death ritual has been a part of the human life cycle for centuries, and, while it may help assuage the pain of the survivors, those whom the rituals center around are well beyond the scope of any kind of solace.

Shaniya's story galvanized every pocket of the nation, first with the energy of hope for her safe return, then in a collective fiery core of outrage at the circumstances surrounding her death. All of this frenetic energy hung in the air, snapping voltage into countless blogs, online memorials and candlelight vigils. And so, O'Neal's contribution became a necessary one. Although her funeral and burial tiptoe around the border of ostentatious, their magnitude only serves to gather the jagged, angry currents of the public's sorrow and offer them an outlet to weep in unity.

Her funeral was crowded with over two thousand in attendance and hundreds more peering into the church through the stained-glass windows. Even Raleigh station WRAL televised parts of it on the evening news. Shaniya's mother, Antoinette Davis, watched bits of it from her jail cell in Raleigh, at the North Carolina Correctional Institute for Women. Pregnant at the time of Shaniya's funeral, she folded her arms over her swollen belly, knowing that her unborn child would be a ward of the State. This unborn child would be lost to her in a completely different way than Shaniya. The birth of Antoinette's last child would be shrouded in the same confusion and chaos that surrounded her second-born's death. The crime, lasting less than two hours in total, left Antoinette childless and her two remaining children without their mother.

Like Shaniya's last trip alive, the little girl's final trip would be in the back of a car, this time as an honored guest. On November 22, 2009, her hearse, followed by a somber processional, crept its way through the cold streets of Fayetteville until they arrived at Shaniya's final destination, the Fayetteville Memorial Cemetery. Her plot lies just off one of the two main winding roads through the cemetery.

And here she will lie under her magnificent and mammoth tombstone until sufficient time passes to allow the elements and the earth to reclaim their own. "And the dust returns to the ground it came from, and the spirit returns to God who gave it," Ecclesiastes 12:7 New International Version (NIV). She lies in good company. Of her 1,206 choices in a neighbor, she rests next to another child, who lies under a Raggedy-Ann-shaped tombstone. Maybe the two of them frolic about the pleasant dirt lanes at night, holding hands and making friends. But such fancies are impossible to imagine when standing in front of Shaniya's heart-shaped tombstone on a hot, bright morning in June. Her face is etched not once but twice into the granite. Carved into the heart shape are the words:

OUR ANGEL CALLED HOME.

Shaniya is smiling in both of her pictures, but her large, serious eyes hold a sad wisdom that betrays her round cheeks and upturned mouth. The tombstone holds a permanent vase for flowers, and among the plastic green stems and yellow and orange and blue fabric of the flowers, someone stuffed two Barbie dolls.

Their presence here is startling; they gaze out at the visitor with unblinking eyes set into their tiny heads, their hair wild and ratty, much like Shaniya's was when she was kidnapped. Antoinette told the 911 operator that her hair was "like a bushy Afro." Shaniya's last known image on the hotel's surveillance video confirmed its wildness. These two Barbie dolls were meant as a playful offering to the dead child but have become like Shaniya, worn and weary, sullied and lifeless. The dolls remain frozen in potential, and their place here is almost mocking, reminding those who walk by this spot that the childish hands that lie just feet away can never reach to play with these two feral dolls. Shaniya is trapped under an insuperable barrier of death and cemented into her place with a memorial stone that serves as a metaphor for her life. The heavy stone, with the word "home" written on it, is too ponderous and too gruesome for the young child to carry. And so she remains in death as she did in life, suffocating under weights and concepts that were never meant for her tiny bones to bear.

There are others lying here, all of them missed and memorialized like Shaniya. Her heart-shaped tombstone is not out of place. It has become fashionable to carve creative headstones, calling attention to the life the stone commemorates. Fayetteville Memorial Cemetery is a repository of artistic tombstones. There are all manner of shapes and memorials, including a granite bicycle tribute and several sites with ornate benches. It is common here, as well, for loved ones to etch photos of the deceased into the tombstone, reminding the world that this body once held the life of a person who smiled and who was loved.

One older boy, buried in a plot that his parents transformed into something closer to a shrine, approached his death from cancer with courage and foresight. Ryan Kishbaugh's illness was long enough that he was able to write his own epitaph, which included the prophetic lines, "I have a premonition that this story will not end in me, but will carry on. . . . I have made a choice to not just be another victim of cancer. . . . Even if it kills me, cancer will never break me. It will never win." But cancer had broken him. How can one remain unbroken in death? His pictures and plaques emphasize the constancy and reliability of death. As moving and delicate as the memorials are, the graveyard remained true to its name, engendering a sense of loss and smallness. Kishbaugh's memorial is on a small hill, and from its vantage point, one can see Shaniya's grave a few sections away. The hundreds of tombstones sandwiched between these two children are a reminder that many of those who rest here were taken by killers who could not be prosecuted. Some children died of disease; others died as victims of another's anger or jealousy or pain. In the end, regardless of the means of dying, death becomes the common denominator of life.

* * *

Thousands of people have left messages on Shaniya's memorial Internet sites, claiming love and devotion. They open with a term of endearment such as, "Hey, lil' mama," or "baby girl" or, most common, "Angel." The visitors go on to express how much they love her and how heaven gained another star, or that Jesus is holding her tightly. The writers of these messages cry nightly tears over her death and promise vindication against those who stole her life. The posts, filled with wishes to Shaniya, only remind the reader that Shaniya is dead. The visitors here write epitaphs pouring empty promises into a computer screen for a child whose life was already broken by too much emptiness and, indeed, held very little promise. To some, these messages are irritating and disturbing. Do their authors love Shaniya? Can they love her? Love is an action of wrenching sacrifice and cannot be equated to a syrupy sentence meant to elevate the sender at the expense of the receiver. Shaniya is remembered, yes; she is a conduit of controversy and judgment, but is she loved? These proclamations, meant to carry such import, float above her heart-shaped tombstone as impotent missives representing judgment against the mother or the killer or the system rather than endearments for the child.

I too have been guilty of having my good intentions directed by obligations. I lived in Atlanta in a wretched warehouse with my children and a team of well-meaning Christians in order to "give my life away for the poor." The warehouse floor we lived on felt active and full of life at the time, but upon retrospect, I see it as chaotic and dangerous. The homeless shelter was one level below us with our floor meant to be used as exclusive housing for those who were serving, not for those who were served.

A mother arrived at the shelter one day. She had two little girls and a young teenage son. They were a ragged lot—torn clothing and a flat look that can only be achieved through true hopelessness. The mother asked to meet with us up on our floor. She was concerned about her son's sleeping conditions that night. She was soft-spoken and the two girls clung to her dirty, buttoned-up shirt. Because he was thirteen, the shelter rules would not allow her male child to sleep in the women and children's section. The shelter, which also served as the church sanctuary, was one long, open room with a cement floor. Sleeping areas were separated out by crinkly plastic blue tarps. Women and children were kept off in a large corner near the bathrooms for safety and practicality. Her son would have been required to sleep in the larger men's section. This worried her. She wanted him to sleep up on our floor in the boy's dorm. She felt he would be safer here among the young Christian missionaries than down among the street sleepers and drug sellers. She could not have been more mistaken.

But because her argument made good sense, we broke with our strict tradition and allowed the child to sleep in the dorm. When we all met up for breakfast the next morning, the mother and the two girls were gone. The boy was panicked, but we were seasoned enough to believe that she had left for a meeting with her Medicaid social worker or some other activity that keeps the poor in exhausting lines filling out exhaustive forms processed by exhausted employees. When she did not return for dinner that night, we joined the child in his alarm. For three days he became our orphaned boy, and we all served as surrogate parents. During those three days, that boy watched our massive, hinged warehouse door slide open and closed, waiting, hoping, believing that his mother was on the other side. On the third day, she and the girls returned from the cat hole that they had buried themselves in. They came in carrying little bags of popcorn, the kind you can buy at Target as you shop the aisles. Apparently, the day she arrived at our shelter was also the day she received her monthly benefit check. With the two, young girls in tow, this mother fed her addiction, leaving just enough money to take the girls on a shopping spree. When the cash was gone, she returned to collect her son. I was livid. This boy was intelligent enough to understand her betrayal and abandonment. As his mother explained her absence in her soft lilt of a voice about needing to buy this or that for the girls, the boy kept his large eyes focused on the popcorn bags that the girls snacked from. He was enraged. "You been gone three days and you didn't bring me any popcorn?" She skirted the question, not even requiring his sisters to share their loot with him. She attempted to assure him by reminding him they were all going to "hit the road tomorrow" on some ill-fated plan to get to Texas.

We told her we would keep him one more night upstairs, and we all tucked in for the night. Breakfast revealed that the three of them had once again slipped away before dawn. I spoke with the boy about it, and he begged me not to call the Department of Social Services. I could practically smell his fear. I made the promise. "You can stay with us as long as you are safe," I assured him, wanting to offer a small comfort in his harsh and desolate life.

He was relieved and said, "You don't know how bad it is when they take you." I wondered how many times he had been "taken" by DSS, but I soon was lost in the endless toil of servitude. Several days passed and she did not return. I became irritated at her cavalier attitude and felt she was taking advantage of me, knowing I would tend to her son while she and the girls had their version of a tea party. In the end, I did not keep my promise to the boy.

The police responded to my call shortly before the mother returned. The boy stared at me as a police officer approached him. Unexpectedly, he bolted, running through the warehouse floor, evading their custody. He was slippery. He kept shouting, "You promised. You promised!" and he ran as if for his life. After a circuitous run around the space with the clumsy police officers behind—the floor was as large as a city block—he made his way to that heavy, hinged door, and I knew he was no match for it. He threw himself against it, all the while screaming at me that I had broken my promise. He frantically pushed at it, scratching at the wood in his desperate attempt to escape. The police approached him gently only after he had expended his rage hurling himself against that unyielding door. They led him downstairs, and I watched from the fire escape as they put him in the back of their car. Even with the car door shut, I could still hear his muffled, "You broke your promise!" screaming out at me. Sometimes, when my mind is quiet and I start to exhale, I can still hear his primal screams of betrayal all these years later.

The boy was right. I had broken my promise. He would have been as safe and cared for with us as he would have been with DSS. The mom would have eventually returned, and who is to say if his life would have been better or worse with her, with us, or in a children's home? All three options presented limitations and failings. We were so wrapped up in the industry and ceaseless toil of the work with the poor that we made her abandonment possible. We felt pretty smug about ourselves for those few nights he stayed under our care. We had taken in the discarded and the lost just as Jesus had asked us to do.

I did not call DSS to assist the child or even out of any great desire to protect him. I called DSS because I was mad at that selfish mother. I was mad on his behalf and mad on my own. I was jealous that she was crafty enough to thrust her son onto an unwitting group of people. I was furious she accepted welfare checks and got to shop at Target and buy popcorn for her girls while we offered free babysitting service. On the surface, my call to DSS looked like one more benevolent act in a long lifetime of similar acts of mercy. But I knew, and the boy knew, that I called them to spite the mother.

So when I read all those messages about heaven and Jesus and puppies on Shaniya's pages, I knew that their messages may hold mercies, but that their hearts could hold judgment. I know now what that boy knew then. No matter how well packaged or how selfless the interference, each action, each broadcast act of compassion, holds the potential for a duplicitous mission of acting as benevolence that simply masks selfishness and sometimes even arrogance. Such acts themselves appear righteous, but the one offering them may be masked in self-righteousness, perhaps even unrecognized, making the actions perform the job of a weapon at the expense of the wounded.

Mercifully, Shaniya can no longer feel the abject physical pain that most assuredly accompanied her death, nor is she subject to the emotional pain that accompanied her life. There is a solace in this. Death, with its final authority, has its say. Shaniya lies here under her mighty tribute, silent and still among the swirl of judgments and hypocrisy that defined her life. Shaniya Davis' life is only remembered and honored because of her death. The space between birth and death is how we describe life. But Shaniya's life, with such a scant amount of time between the two, is not restrained by the conditions of her birth, any more than she is contained by the conditions of her death. Her death serves as a symbol of all that is rotten and wicked within humanity. And yet, in the innocence of her life, she becomes a talisman of all that is pure and good and hopeful within us.

Just as I am, and waiting not
To rid my soul of one dark blot;
To Thee whose blood can cleanse each spot,
O Lamb of God, I come, I come!
– Charlotte Elliot
1834 hymn *"Just as I am"*

Fraud

AT FIRST GLANCE, this might appear to be a story about Antoinette Davis, one of the most hated women in America. Antoinette is a convicted felon. She is considered the worst type of offender, with convictions including sexual servitude of a minor, rape and murder. Her crimes are shocking and incite unquantifiable amounts of animosity and rage. I am drawn to her story, compelled to it even. Like the rest, I want to understand who she is and how this happened. But what keeps me submerged in this uncomfortable and heavy ocean is the need to understand *why*. Why Antoinette and not me?

It is wildly unpopular to examine oneself against a convicted felon. I have been taught to believe in a binary system of *good* and therefore, *bad*. Initially, I saw myself as good, and therefore, Antoinette as bad. But through choices and decisions, I could be one or the other. I have always questioned these definitive boundaries. My own life experience taught me, for example, that a father could be both a church leader and a pedophile, and this knowledge hurled me into the interstitial where I happily live my life. Here, in the middle, in my in-between, I understand that there are infinite choices between good and bad and that even defining these outlying terms leads to probabilities and conditions that blur the distinctions between the two. On any given day, I am both immeasurably good and kind and loving and even pure in some moments while also deceitful, abjectly selfish, and sometimes even criminal in others.

Should I be convicted of a felony, it would be for the crime of fraud. I fraudulently present a person to the world who is sometimes in direct conflict with the person in my heart. My defrauded Facebook page would read like Antoinette's series of convictions. True status lines would go beyond "My son is brilliant" to include "but dropped out of high school." Further, "I love my wonderful husband" would transform to "but fear he is sometimes bored in our marriage." My fraud-free Facebook would reveal, "I willed my friend's house to burn down," and "I am jealous of every girl with thin arms," or "I want to castrate most men I know." The human I present to the world behaves well and smiles a lot. The human I keep caged within my heart is a liar and profoundly scared most of the time.

Yes, I hear the objections: "But Antoinette was accused of selling her daughter to cover a $200 drug debt." Heinous. Yes. Horrifying, unquestionably. But here, in the grey area of the interstitial, I argue that my crimes against humanity are as heinous and as horrifying. I was able to tame my monster, and have learned, through privilege or wit—or perhaps it was luck—to present my more saintly qualities to the world. But if I am to honestly seek the *why* in Antoinette, I must also confess to the commonality of our humanity. This book is a slow exposure of the cancerous sins that I have committed which, aside from luck and circumstance, define me as similar to Antoinette. She is monster and saint, just as I am. We are both exceptional and ordinary. We are everything and we are nothing and we are all things in-between.

Chocolate Milk

DEATH INTRODUCED ITSELF early in my childhood, and we have held a reciprocated interest in each other ever since. When I attended Lohr Elementary School in Canton, Ohio, an older boy, a fifth grader, died during recess. Our teachers were unprepared for this death, here, in the middle of a primary school playground. Death was not something they were taught to teach. There was some sort of whisper through the school that caught hold of our classroom like a vapor. My twin sister, who was in a different class across the hall, said her class was talking about it that afternoon as well. But my classroom's windows overlooked the playground where the little boy had died, and we were drawn to the scene, not fully understanding what we were witnessing. Our classroom was on the ground floor, putting us level with the action. Our teacher stood among us, staring out at a cluster of adults gathered around a small boy. The room was hushed, and even as young children, we knew we were watching something that was not meant to be seen.

Just before the ambulance arrived, our teacher collected herself and quickly closed the blinds. We were ushered to our seats and told to put our heads down onto our desks. I can't recall if we started another lesson or if we were still sitting with our heads down when our classroom door opened noisily. We all glanced back to see who was coming in. It was our lunch lady in a pink smock rolling in trays of milk on a school cart that normally held the filmstrip projectors. The row captains were told to collect and distribute the milk cartons to each child in the row. All the milk cartons were white with red lettering but for one solitary carton. It was brown with white writing, which meant it was chocolate. I wanted it.

My row captain collected five white cartons and passed them out to each of our eager hands. But I kept an eye on that chocolate milk and saw the lunch lady hand it to a particular captain, whispering something in her ear. I opened my own milk, excited that we got such an unexpected treat in the middle of the school day. I had almost forgotten about the playground and all the adults scurrying around on the other side of our closed windows. The captain with the chocolate milk walked to her row and handed a milk to each child. She had two cartons left, one chocolate and one white; she handed the chocolate milk to Ricky Montgomery. He put the milk on his desk but did not open it. Other kids in the class must have been watching that coveted chocolate milk as well because one of them whispered, "Hey! That's Ricky's brother." Our classmate was gesturing toward the darkened blinds. "That's Ricky's brother out there on the playground." I whipped my head back to stare at Ricky. I was thinking of a way I could get his attention to trade my milk for his when Ms. Billie, our pretty, blond-haired teacher, walked down the row housing Ricky, helped him get up and escorted him to the lunch lady, who walked him out of our classroom. He left his milk sitting on his desk.

It was commonly known around our community that Ricky's brother was an ill child born with a faulty heart and his early death had been dreaded, but anticipated by his family long before it arrived. Ricky was out of school for a few days, and when he returned, none of us talked to him about it. We just acted as if it had never occurred. But we never forgot. Through the rest of my years at the elementary school, many of the kids, including myself, made a big show of walking around the spot where Ricky's older brother had collapsed and then died. Nobody was brave enough to step on it.

From the moment we all crowded up against that wall of windows, my fascination with death was aroused. Up to this point, Ricky's older brother was the first and only body I had ever seen that wasn't old, dressed up and displayed in a funeral home. I can remember with perfect clarity how his body lay on the black pavement. He fell down near the handball court just a few feet away from the tetherball post. I didn't see any blood, just Ricky's brother crumpled up on the playground with adults running toward him. In my mind, these events are cemented solidly, and each detail from the time we were shooed away from the window to Ricky Montgomery's exit from our classroom, remains an acute memory.

After Ricky left, there was a let-down in the room. The slow-motion events that occurred in those twenty minutes were full of intrigue and urgency. I was intensely aware of each detail: I had a snag on one of my cotton knee socks; one of the Elmer's glue bottles in the window had tipped over, forming a tiny puddle of white that had dried to the orange tip. Mark Brown was wearing a brown shirt, which I had found funny at the beginning of the day. Everything dragged on slowly and impossibly fast all at once. This acute sentience felt like a pang of a particular type of pleasure that later became intoxicating. We had watched death through a window, and the subsequent distancing and silencing around this event pushed our experience into *forbidden* and *secret*. I wanted to shout away the whispers and shine some light of understanding into the dark, forbidden place.

The row captains passed the trash can back for us to discard our cartons. Ricky's captain pushed his unopened milk into the trashcan without a thought. Something special had happened to us, but we could tell from Ms. Billie's demeanor that we were not meant to discuss it. It was a bad thing, I learned, to covet the chocolate milk of a boy whose brother had died under our watchful eyes. And it was very much a worse thing, to open conversation or ask questions about what we had shared that day. Our class was connected by this event. Strangely, Ricky, on the fault line of the after-shocks, was excluded from our experience. I learned that those who are in the center of a death storm become ostracized by the lucky ones who merely watch the effects of the howling wind from the safety of shelter. We were fascinated by it, yes, but we also distanced ourselves from Ricky. The observers always have an advantage over the observed. There was a certain quiet power here and I wanted more of it.

The Bustle in a House
The Morning after Death
Is solemnest of industries
Enacted upon Earth –

The Sweeping up the Heart
And putting Love away
We shall not want to use again
Until Eternity –
                – Emily Dickinson circa 1850

Voyeurism

THIS EVENT RUMBLED a hunger in me. I felt alive and a part of something sacred. A group of us had watched a boy die and now were covertly encouraged to make it a secret. I wasn't especially drawn to the dying itself, but rather to the mechanisms surrounding death, the bustle in our house. The teachers wouldn't discuss it, and, after a few meaningful hugs, our parents were eager to dismiss it as well. We were all captivated by it, but social rules dictated that we not openly acknowledge it. My own childhood house was full of industry so solemn I sometimes longed for death. But it had also encouraged me to seek satisfaction outside its rigid walls. So, after the death of Ricky's brother, I looked to feed my hunger in the only place left in Perry Township that offered the nourishment I sought. I went to the Stark County Public Library. It was an unassuming building nestled between the middle school and high school but I learned its secrets that summer. I'd examine the spines of each book and each one whispered back to me. Voyeurism was not only required here but was also celebrated. The library's rows of books felt like arms reaching to comfort, to inform, to entice. I found in the library what all lonely kids search for there; I found companionship.

I began with fictional crime. I read every book available in our little town's library. I devoured the juvenile fiction books and quickly turned my attention to the adult section. But this proved more problematic. The Stark County Public Library held to a very strict policy of not allowing minors to check out books from the adult section. One librarian in particular, Peggy, seemed gratified beyond the expected measure each time she denied me as I approached her with my carefully chosen stack of adult crime fiction books. I even tried to hide the adult fiction in between obvious juvenile books, but she was on to me. I took to hiding between the shelves in the library, furtively reading the prohibited books as if I was covering up a crime of my own.

My interest was diverted from the library as my own childhood home demanded my full attention and dedicated concentration in order to endure. Years passed and when I was finally able to escape my hometown, I traveled far into the South to thaw my bones from the long, bitter winter that was my childhood.

I was already bored with fictional crime stories by this time and had turned to newspaper articles about true crime. True crime held the advantages that fiction could not offer. For one, there was the introduction of the justice system. None of the books I read offered many details about criminal courts and testimonies. The newspaper articles featured exacting details from the trials, even adding actual excerpts from testimonies. These quoted words enticed me. Reading these stories put me right back into that elementary school window. I was permitted to safely watch the narrative from an endorsed seat. The newspaper stories, and later, the Internet swarm of stinging information, allowed me to investigate true crimes without reproach. I feasted on these stories, often hunting down court transcripts to scratch some unreachable itch down in my consciousness.

Another advantage of true crime stories was the photographs. The illustrations provided by the publishers in my fictional world never quite captured the images I had created in my head. I found the illustrations a distraction from the words. But in nonfiction, in those newspaper articles and more so on the Internet, there were actual photographs of murder weapons and bad men. I stared into the vacant and sometimes menacing gaze of all those mug shots. There was an arrogance present that would evaporate once the gavel fell on *guilty*. I loved looking at the pictures of the convicted men in shackles and orange jumpsuits. The photographs provided an accurate visual landscape upon which I could frame the words themselves. Unlike the distraction of fictional illustrations, the photographs abetted me in my understanding of the stories. And so I developed a life-long propensity toward reading and researching non-fiction crimes. Once the Internet became available, I was able to luxuriate over an endless search for the next good crime story and there was no Peggy wagging her sanctioned disapproval.

There were millions of us gazing into other people's catastrophes and in those millions, I found my lost classmates who witnessed a tragedy in a collective trance of fascinated horror. I wanted to recapture that sharp, intoxicating experience of being aware I had back in that elementary school classroom. It was just a matter of time before I would find Antoinette Davis.

I am not macabre enough to consider my front seat window into death as a lucky event, but I do feel my passive participation observing the details surrounding that child's death as prophetic, forecasting thousands of hours to armchair researching of crimes, watching true crime shows and reading court transcripts as an adult. I have nursed a crush on NBC's *Dateline* host Keith Morrison for years.

In my experience, people in prison show an alarming eagerness to tell their story, to set the record straight. I never anticipated such a lengthy and fortified caution (from Antoinette) or antagonism (from Dollie Bray, defense team). I thought speaking with Antoinette would be the easy part.

Murderpedia

I STARTED AT *Murderpedia,* a free, online encyclopedia of murderers, because I was comfortable there; its tabs and forums were as cozy as my own living room. I knew I wanted to write a story about a murder, but there were too many here. I would have to narrow my search significantly. I have never been interested in female murderers, mostly choosing to believe that they were either framed or justified. Additionally, serial killers do not hold my attention. This left me with thousands of male murderers to wade through.

Murderpedia lists the felons alphabetically and each click on a letter reveals up to three hundred names. My parameters for research were still much too large. I must narrow my focus. I wanted the crime to have occurred in North Carolina. I wanted to research and write about a crime that had only one victim. Spree killers or thrill killings were off the list because my desire was to investigate a murder that held some kind of meaning around it—sociopaths or addicts murdered without a reasonable connection to the victim. I faced the *Murderpedia* home page with my mouse poised above the "As," wanting to be thorough and comprehensive in my choice. It took me hours to get through the letter "B" but nothing stood out to me. I didn't feel connected to any of the crimes or the victims or they didn't meet my research requirements. Grad school had taught that proper research must lack empathy. *Logos* was the battle cry leaving *Pathos* outside the classroom door. This appealed to my sensibilities. I have long found emotion a diversion to reasonable thinking. Even when my young children were still adorable, I would dismiss the cute pouty lip of "Pleeease" in favor of a logical argument. Those salty tears dripping from large little girl eyes could not sway me, but an evidential argument, even if housed in childlike language, could.

My personality allowed me to summarily dismiss the stories of those who had lost their lives based on the steady characters that trample human integrity: betrayal, greed and lust. I read the stories of thousands of murder victims through the years, but none of their sad stories compelled me to research further than the cursory facts of the crime. I began to wonder if my "stoic" approach to choosing a creditable murder story would eliminate all potential candidates. But I was determined to write like Ann Rule, a celebrated nonfiction crime writer, detailing a true crime story with integrity and intelligence, and so I kept scrolling and scanning.

I was a few hours into the Bs when it suddenly occurred to me to start in the middle of the alphabet. I got the idea from Harlan Ellison's short story "'Repent, Harlequin,' Said the Ticktock Man." He opens his narrative with, "Begin in the middle, and later, learn the beginning, and the rest will take care of itself." Hoping for some good-luck-Ellison juju, I skipped to the Ms, not in a Ouija board kind of a way, but more in a determined, convicted kind of way.

I scrolled through the letter, rejecting those men who did not fit my parameters when I stopped on a man from North Carolina named Jeffrey Robert MacDonald. He was convicted of murdering his wife and their two little girls. It was a compelling story. MacDonald, a Princeton graduate who later became a doctor, initially told police that three masked intruders had overtaken him while he was lounging on the family sofa. I liked that he broke the "murderer stereotype" in that he was educated, white and wealthy. He claimed that one of the men punctured his lung with an ice pick and subdued him with his own pajama top while the other attackers ran into the bedrooms, stabbing his little girls and his wife to death. MacDonald wrestled his pajama top around his hands to ward off further stabbing attempts by his assailant.

Much would be made of the type of puncture wounds to the fabric in trial. While he wrestled the armed attacker, the baby girl, just 2 years old, was stabbed fifteen times with a knife in addition to thirty-three stab wounds with an ice pick. It's hard to imagine that the 2-year-old's tiny body would be large enough to contain so many puncture wounds. MacDonald's wife, Colette, who was pregnant with their third child at the time of her murder, was clubbed and beaten so badly that both of her arms were broken. She was stabbed thirty-seven times with both weapons. Here is where MacDonald's testimony about his pajama top proves important. That top was found with twenty-one punctures in the fabric. This is the same number of puncture wounds that were inflicted upon Mrs. MacDonald through the aforementioned pajama top. The murderer had draped it across her chest and stabbed her twenty-one times through it. All twenty-one of these stab wounds were inflicted upon her body postmortem.

Once he had spent his rage, the murderer dipped his surgically gloved hand into her pooling blood and wrote the word "pig" on the headboard. The police accusing MacDonald believed this was in an attempt to corroborate his story that three "hippie type" adults had entered his home intent on murder. Just one foot away from where MacDonald had lounged on the sofa was an *Esquire* magazine covering the story about Charles Manson and the Tate murders. Police believed MacDonald had written "pig" on the headboard to cast suspicion off himself. But the forensic evidence proved his downfall. Both of the girls had fibers of his much discussed pajama top under their bodies, and there was even a thread of it found under his wife's fingernails. He maintained his innocence and, in fact, twenty years later did not apply for parole because it would require him to accept responsibility for the crime. Despite expert testimony, forensic evidence and my own bias that men are likely guilty, I still find it difficult to dismiss cases where the defendant insists on his innocence so many years after the conviction.

I did not pursue this case because the crime happened in 1970 and I felt that I could not properly research, certainly not to the rigorous standards of my grad school professor, Dr. Assidon, who recommended access to primary documents. Most of the participating parties had moved away or forgotten the details. Additionally, I would be required to study two trial transcripts. MacDonald was initially tried in military court where he was found "Not Guilty." His father-in-law, a rigid and unflappable believer in MacDonald's innocence during the first trial, began to find his behavior suspicious. He would later encourage local prosecutors to pursue MacDonald. State prosecution is not bound by double jeopardy laws if the case was heard in a military courtroom. This left MacDonald open to a Grand Jury Indictment which then led to his second trial. In his civilian trial, MacDonald's verdict did not end so well. He was found guilty and given three life sentences, which he is serving consecutively in the Federal prison in Cumberland, Maryland. Besides that, I eliminated MacDonald from my list because I did not want to interact with anything related to the military. Additionally, while MacDonald's opened a solid discussion of his guilt or innocence, something I wanted, I *believed* him to be guilty, something I did not want. As I poured through *Murderpedia* and other sites (they are numerous), I was reminded that we are a people capable of great violence even as we exhibit great forgiveness.

There were other murderers from North Carolina whom I summarily rejected based on arbitrary issues. For example, I could not easily pronounce George Marecek's victim's name or that of his Thai wife, Viparet Marecek. I did find it noteworthy that both MacDonald and Marecek served in the Green Berets, but this was likely due to my search limitation of crimes that occurred in North Carolina. I wanted the research portion of the book to be close to my home in Asheville. Fort Bragg is a large military base between Sanford and Fayetteville, North Carolina, so perhaps it makes sense that trained soldiers were more apt to commit crimes. This military base houses US Special Forces including the CIA's aptly titled "Special Actions Division" (SAD). Both MacDonald and Marecek served at Fort Bragg. President Kennedy visited the base in 1960 with the specific purpose of honoring the Green Berets. George Marecek and

Jeffrey MacDonald were among those who stood before him to receive this honor. Marecek's story was complicated, like MacDonald's, which I liked, but problematic in that part of the case involved a love affair with a woman in the Czech Republic and there were political overtones of Communism throughout the trial. Popular opinion at the time held that Marecek was a Soviet spy.

Like MacDonald, Marecek stood trial more than once. His first trial ended in a hung jury with the second finding him guilty of first degree murder. He successfully appealed and won the right to a third trial, where he was found guilty again but had his original thirty-year sentence diminished by half. Marecek was paroled in 2003 and was quietly absorbed back into civilian life. There were elements of the story that appealed to me. I liked the detail of his wife watching *All My Children* on the day of the murder and that she chose low fat cottage cheese for her lunch. It would be her final meal. I wonder if she wished she had gone for something fatty and satisfying like lasagna or a grilled ham and cheese sandwich. It's unlikely she had time to consider it in that she was unexpectedly bludgeoned and, when that proved ineffective, drowned just a few hours after her healthy, and likely disappointing lunch. The murder was intriguing even if the motive was predictable, but this idea of Marecek as a Soviet spy was beyond my area of competence. And I did not want to get tangled up in Military Court documents. I suspected that even with the Freedom of Information Act, I would run into roadblocks that would delay my goal of completing the manuscript within six months of the commencement of research. This belief in the relative ease of securing public documents would prove, of course, to be a naïve assumption, but at the time it was sufficient enough for me to move down the list of male murderers in North Carolina.

I passed on several North Carolinian Ms, including Ernest Paul McCarver. McCarver was an easy reject for me in that he had blond hair and a shaggy beard, both objectionable offenses against my own proclivities. And so it went, name after name, betrayal after betrayal with me dipping into some stories with a full splash and others cautiously wading about on the periphery. It was either a matter of elimination or a sharp shove of fate that caused me to fall into the story of Mario McNeill.

Mario Andretti

AT FIRST GLANCE, it was his name that drew me in: Mario Andretti McNeill. Around the same time Ricky's brother died at school, Mario Andretti, the famous race car driver, was zipping around cement racetracks, winning prestigious first place trophies in all kinds of big money competitions. My interest in Andretti began and ended with the knowledge that he had a twin brother, Aldo. Because I was a twin myself, I was always fascinated with other sets.

Growing up in the gentle farmland of Ohio that pushed up against Indiana, many people in our community were fans of the Indianapolis 500, based solely on its close proximity. The boys in our neighborhood gang raced each other up and down Hurless Drive on their bikes, pretending to be in race cars. My uncle, in particular, watched the car races from his modest living room sofa, shushing my sister and me from our noisy chatter. We spent thousands of hours under his safe and inviting roof with our cousins. The mosquito sound of those cars whining around the endless circle became a familiar backdrop to the happier moments of our childhood.

So, when my eyes scanned Mario Andretti McNeill's name on the *Murderpedia* list, my heart gave a slight nod of recognition that caused me to linger. I clicked on McNeill's name and was immediately captivated by his dreadlocks and vacant eyes. He looked like a scary, bad man. I wanted to know his story.

In the Beginning

THE CRIME ITSELF took just over two hours from inception to completion. Of course those one hundred and twenty minutes cannot be understood on their own. One cannot scoop out a bucket of water and claim to hold the river itself. These minutes descend from a powerful waterfall involving several people over the course of almost an entire generation. Isolated, these minutes reveal a tragic and complex story that begins like all stories of this nature—in the darkest portions of a human heart. The crime is driven by the familiar current of lust, control, greed and betrayal. But this crime has happened before, thousands of times in as many years. It is not to humanity's credit that such crimes have been occurring since seconds after the primordial ooze shaped itself into a human soul.

The official statement regarding this crime involves action verbs that have no business smashed up against the nouns they follow. A little girl was sold by her mother to cover a drug debt. The child was raped, murdered and discarded until her body was found six days later. That's the short version.

The historic version can be found within the first book of the Bible. Cain murders his brother Abel by chapter four of Genesis. Twenty-six chapters later is the first recorded Biblical rape when little Dinah, just barely a teenager, is raped by the son of a city official. Her brother Joseph is sold by his brothers into a human trafficking ring where he becomes a slave in Egypt by chapter forty-three. Abraham himself participated in sexual servitude when he "had relations" with his wife's servant, Hagar, with the sole intention of birthing a son. It's not surprising, then, to find Abraham's own nephew, Lot, in an attempt to protect his house guest, bargaining with the rowdy, drunken fraternity party held on the other side of his zippered tent by offering to send out his virgin daughters. The girls were spared this violation only to birth their own father's children several verses later. Nancy Grace wasn't around to call these crimes "despicable" as she had done in Shaniya's case, nor was there the level-headed, inspiring voice of Oprah Winfrey who added her evaluation to this narrative by allowing Lockhart and those like him as guests on her show.

But the person at the center of these events is not the person who committed the crimes. The woman at the center of the one hundred and twenty minutes in question did not murder and did not rape. Nevertheless, Antoinette Nicole Davis is one of the most despised women in America. Her criminal record, based on the events of a cold morning in November 2009, exposes a dark and disturbing story that captured the media's attention from her first 911 call to her conviction four years later.

> "The sum of the square roots of any two sides of an isosceles triangle is equal to the square root of the remaining side. Oh, joy! Oh, rapture! I've got a brain!"
> – Scarecrow
> in *The Wizard of Oz*

Pythagorean Theorem

LIKE SCARECROW, I approached this devastating story with a dimwitted understanding of the triangulation of this crime. There was Mario McNeill holding up one side, little Shaniya Davis on the other, and my book would explore the third side, Antoinette Davis. Pythagoras had an idea back in Ancient Greece that explored understanding an unknown by defining the known. He created a theorem that proves the square of two sides of a triangle will produce the hypotenuse of the third. The hypotenuse is the longest side of a right triangle. I saw this crime as two intersecting points, McNeill and the child as held together by the longer side, Antoinette. That longer side was the unknown.

I felt I clearly understood what a McNeill was. As a society, we may not understand the psychology behind pedophilia, but we certainly understand that it exists. Additionally, we have a clear perception of the personality behind a small-time neighborhood drug dealer. At best, McNeill was a hoodlum; at worst, he was a predator. So in 2009, when McNeill awakened Shaniya Davis from the sofa inside the trailer that she called home, carried her into the cold November morning, transported her to a cheap hotel almost forty minutes away, raped, asphyxiated and finally dumped her little body into an animal graveyard, society understood exactly who he was. The community and the nation rushed to find justice for the little girl.

Some speculate that her status of mixed race—her mother a black woman, her father a white man—is what pushed her story into a media sensation. There were those in the small town of Fayetteville, North Carolina, who felt that if Shaniya had not been biologically connected to a white father, her murder would not have raised such a national media frenzy. But it's unlikely those claims can be substantiated. The values and opinions of the modern population had already been reflected in new legislation that defined pedophilia as a criminal act and pedophiles as unforgivable malefactors. Shaniya's race remained irrelevant in the face of such a heartbreaking crime. McNeill kidnapped a child from the place where she, arguably, should have been the safest and the most protected. He sexually violated her on a filthy, hotel room comforter, then, using his hands in an act more intimately violating than the rape itself, he asphyxiated her.

So we understand McNeill's side of the triangle. He was a hoodlum, neighborhood drug dealer who sexually preyed upon the children of those addicted to his product. And then he murdered a girl. The only way to draw his line in this story is straightforward, no unexpected twists, no deep mystery. He lived the life of a habitual criminal until his line smashed into the child's, forming a collision that caused both of them to lose their lives in the fallout of that intersection. McNeill was a known variable.

The same could be said for Shaniya Davis. Although her life was complicated by both her parents' betrayal, she remained an integral within the triangle. Her line was shorter, yes, but it served as an inverse parallel to McNeill's. While his line was drawn with dark, criminal intentions, hers was a life-line of light and purity. Shaniya necessarily became a representation of innocence and joy, her long, 5-year-old legs stretching out gracefully in white stockings peeking out from a pink tutu. Shaniya could not be fully known, in that she had so little time to define her personhood, but she could be fully understood. She was an innocent. An innocent who was dragged mercilessly into a configuration that would first shatter and then destroy her.

If old Pythagoras was correct, I expected that a thorough treatment of the two known sides would produce an accurate and reliable understanding of the third. Antoinette Davis, when dropped into the configuration with the monster McNeill and her violated daughter provided a formation of intrigue. She became the hypotenuse, the long side of the story. But nothing is ever that simple. Davis, cloaked in her crimes like a supervillain, lurks about this story on a complicated path, with her actions and presence never fully arriving at the location in the triangle I had mapped out for her. Like Scarecrow, I misapplied the theorem.

Alpha Dog

Antoinette Davis is the first born of Priscilla Ann's children, all of whom were born in Fayetteville, North Carolina. Priscilla was just 16 when she birthed Antoinette. In addition to having a teenage mother, Antoinette was also raised under the cloud that shadows the fatherless.

Although Priscilla presents varying accounts of Antoinette's father, there is a general agreement among those in her family that he is dead. Depending on the rendition, he was either dead during her pregnancy or died shortly after Antoinette's birth. As Priscilla recounts it, Robin Willis was murdered. Priscilla claims Antoinette's father was a sexual player, according to Antoinette, which appears evident considering the circumstances of his murder. At or around the time of Priscilla's delivery of Antoinette, Robin Willis was having an affair with a woman married to a military man who was absent from the home for long stretches of time. It remains unclear how the army man found out about his wife and her lover, but no one disputes the fact that once he was informed, he became enraged.

The husband spotted Willis walking down the sidewalk. Willis remained completely unaware that his lover's husband had returned from deployment. The husband, seeing Willis as an enemy, used his army training to hunt and destroy him. The jilted husband veered his car into a direct collision with Willis. But Willis was plucky. The impact did not result in the desired outcome. So this trained soldier backed up his car and rammed into Willis a second time. In some accounts, this backing up and re-ramming occurred a third time before the soldier declared his "mission accomplished." But some of these facts cannot be verified. Antoinette's mother told her, from her earliest memories, that this vehicular homicide was the fate of her no-good, cheating father. But this was her mother's story. It was challenged by other family members who claim to have known her father.

Because I am a rigidly trained researcher, I chased these facts into intellectual exhaustion. I was formally taught the methods and theories of research in graduate school. I incorrectly assumed grad school would stroke my ego in the same way undergrad had done. In undergrad I sat and raised my hand with the most enthusiasm and secretly raced the other students to turn in my exams. I metaphorically sewed the letter "S" for *scholar* onto my garments to mark myself as set apart from my community. I was an intellectual.

But I was not as successful with the games in graduate school. All the students raised their hands enthusiastically, and many of them offered worthy responses. But they also spoke an erudite language that I felt unable even to imitate, much less acquire. Their speech involved an intricate dance of self-deprecation that was a ruse to achieve self-aggrandizement. They used sentences like, "I'm not certain I remember this passage correctly, but Friedrich Nietzsche said . . ."

Each reference to great thinkers and writers was a coded language that, at its common denominator, said simply, "I am intelligent and you are a dolt." At first, I endeavored to decipher the code by attempting to systemize their references. For example, I noted that the more obscure the reference, the deeper the intellectual distance between sender and receiver.

Deepening these distances, creating this gap, seemed to be the purpose behind the classroom discussions, indeed, behind graduate school itself. But beyond a few surface observations, I was never able to master the language. I kept my "S" attached to my breast, but changed the symbol to stand for *shamed*. I was able to limp across the podium, and, today, I hold my rolled-up diploma as one of my most prized accomplishments. But I was never one of them. I was *among* them but not *of* them. So too, stood Antoinette Davis, wearing her symbolic letter of shame to represent her situation of poverty rather than her condition as human. If I am to see myself as more than *shamed*, then I must be willing to view Antoinette as more than *villain*. There must be more to each of us than the surface representation of our failures. Many times the character of highly successful and deeply esteemed individuals masks darker and more sinister natures.

One of my grad school professors successfully concealed from her colleagues and peers everything I loathed in higher education: she was bloated with her own intelligence and worked to keep education exclusively among "her kind." This professor was well loved in the department, leaving me to feel that I alone saw through her charade.

I have found that insecurity often leads to power; Dr. Assidon was powerful. Unfortunately, my deep level of antipathy toward her was evenly reciprocated from her toward me. Graduate school is a kennel for well-trained dogs who can perform intelligent tricks. Dr. Assidon was an alpha dog, the growling thoroughbred compared to my yelping mutt. But she knew how to orchestrate a dog fight. She would offer us a scant suggestion of a fact and let us loose in the library to fight each other for research documents attempting to substantiate it. It was an intense competition, but those who dragged the dead body of authenticated proof back to her received their reward of a cherished grade.

I was never ranked in the top of the class. Indeed, I hobbled out of her class with a subpar grade, but that grade did not represent all I learned in the dusty pit of rivalry. The professor would sit on the sidelines, often sipping a glass of wine, reminiscent of the entitled audience watching gladiators use savage strategy to stay alive. Students wrestled it out in our arena of the research section of the library. Many times I would pant up to my professor with what I thought was solid factual confirmation only to be dismissed with a pat on the head reserved for the runt of the litter. "That is too broad, too large a scope for the assignment. Go back and narrow it down to find the original source," she would scold. And so she taught me tenacity and a dogged pursuit of worthy, scholarly, tight research. Dr. Assidon would hardly consider my current project worthy or scholarly, but when it concerned research, I was an old dog now, and unable to learn new tricks.

I applied Dr. Assidon's training to narrowing down and ferreting out the truth regarding Antoinette's father. Antoinette once told me that at one time she had Willis' death certificate in her possession. She counted it as one of her prized possessions. It offered her legitimacy by providing tangible evidence of an intangible concept.

But, like others in poverty, Antoinette participated in that slow parade of upheaval, moving from house to house with no true direction or purpose. During one of those moves, Antoinette lost the death certificate long before she moved to Sleepy Hollow, a house that would hold a story connected to another death certificate, one that she would not be permitted to keep.

I was never able to find her father's death certificate. The Robin Willis I did ferret out put his date of death at eighteen years old. This seemed too young to have been that unlucky in choosing a lover. Despite the lack of authentication, no one in the family disputes that Antoinette grew up without a father. There was a trickle of men who ran through her childhood home, but none would stay longer than the time it took to "smoke and relax for a while," as Antoinette remembers it. The smoking referred to crack and the relaxing referred to smokers having sex with her mother. How these two verbs were attached could fuel lofty conversations with the grad school gang. Was it a causal relationship? If so, was the smoking the cause of the relaxing or the relaxing the cause of the smoking? The police considered the association an exchange, making the verbs criminal when put in either order. But despite the temporary but consistent intrusion of men walking through her childhood home, Antoinette grew up orphaned by a man who was meant to play the role of father. There were men *among* her, but they were not *of* her.

Titanic

ANTOINETTE HAD BEEN fatherless for three years when her mother became pregnant with her second child, Sarah. Not long afterward, Priscilla's last born, Brenda, joined her sisters in a world that, by now, Antoinette knew to be unpredictable and scary. Brenda soon became the darling of the family. Her grandparents doted on the child, bringing her new shoes and dresses while Antoinette looked on. Antoinette describes, "My family played favorites and Brenda was the favorite." I asked her if it was because she was the youngest and she replied, "I don't know why, but the whole family babied her." The two younger girls would get scooped up by the grandparents for weeks at a time to stay in their little country home. Antoinette was never invited to these adventures. But the favoritism was short-lived in that once Priscilla lost custody of her girls, they were tossed into a culture of turbulence that served as an equalizer.

My own experience provided a unique slant on the favorite-child syndrome common in so many families. My clan consisted of a grandmother and grandfather who lived geographically and emotionally close to their four children and then grandchildren. It was a tightly wound group of six adults and seven grandchildren all twisted up into each other's houses and lives. Our family culture held deeply to the old-fashioned notions of male glorification and female subjugation. Under this belief system, the family unit suffered a devastating blow when our mother, Caroline, gave birth to twin girls, my sister and me. Girls were already listed on the deficit side of the ledger, but to birth two at one time was considered especially outrageous. Caroline continued this streak of rebellion, eventually executing what no woman in the family before her had accomplished. She abandoned her family; she cut her limb from the family tree. But in the dust kicked up from the severing, there was an aroma of hope. Several years later, we called upon the memory of her daring act to successfully plan an escape of our own. Caroline's greatest contribution in parenting was imparted in her action of quitting the job. This was not the case, however, for Antoinette.

Priscilla was legally severed from her children, but DSS oversight was short-sighted. The girls were placed with their grandmother, allowing Priscilla indiscriminate access, the freedom to roam within and around the home as it was her own mother's property. Antoinette remembers her mom "showing up" despite the court ruling that she have limited contact. Antoinette was never certain when her mom would come around. She both desired and dreaded these unannounced drop-ins.

My sister and I were able to count on Caroline's definitive absence and were therefore spared the pain felt by Antoinette and her younger sisters. Antoinette spent her childhood in that purgatory common to children with an absent parent. She was emotionally arrested in this space of unknowing. My twin and I were able to grieve and then accept Caroline's departure. We were free to grow emotionally from that place of betrayal and rejection. We found solace in the hopelessness of Caroline's return. Not so for Antoinette. She lived in the consistent and ever-present pain associated with hope.

But before Caroline left, she attempted to wrestle out her pain by distributing it between my twin and me. Regardless of her elevation of one twin over the other, we considered it an assault on *us*. Things were less complicated with our father, Glen. He disliked both of us with measured equality. This type of consistency is easier for a child to understand and navigate. Caroline, however, showed a dislike for our *twinship*. She seemed to resent or despise, I could never determine which, the fact that we were twins. She went through a short phase of attempting to divide us. Had Caroline understood the nature of twins in general, and our propensities in particular, she would have abandoned her plan immediately. My sister and I were not just biologically bound by the egg we once shared and then split. We were entwined through our mutual experience as we participated in a horror show of childhood, sometimes as actor, sometimes as audience. This type of shared exploitation produces a bond that cannot be riven. The more Caroline tugged to pull us away from one another, the more intently we clung together.

When she found her efforts were ineffective, she shifted her focus. She began a short-lived but deliberate campaign to dislike my sister. Perhaps *deliberate* is too harsh here. It is possible, probable even, that she did not understand what she was doing. She grew up with adopted parents and maybe it was our identical DNA that scratched her the wrong way. First she picked on and punished my sister at a disproportionate rate more than my brother or me.

But most alarming was her calculated elevation of me. Having been inculcated into the family's belief system of my gender's iniquities, I was unprepared to receive any kind of affirmation. I was female and therefore beneath notice. Our beloved grandfather, the indisputable patriarch, made a family joke out of his wife. "Ah, shut up woman," he would say with such frequency that many of the younger children uttered it among their first phrases. The result of their infantile imitation produced my grandfather and uncle's knee-slapping laughter between bites of butter pecan ice-cream topped with Super Sugar Crisp cereal that was prepared, served and cleaned up by the females.

Once, when we forgot to empty the dehumidifier in the basement—a job we detested because it sat next to a dark, damp, well room that gurgled indiscriminately—our grandpa stood over us as we mopped up the overflowing water. "You girls are just so stupid," he said. This was not meant as a chastisement, but more as a proclamation. "You just don't think," he quietly added, shaking his head at our inept gender. We silently nodded in agreement as we wiped up the water, the stony, cement floor imprinting into our knees a tangible talisman of his message.

Caroline's efforts were less effective. She was certainly mean to my sister, but she lacked the male family trait of cruelty. But from her phase of playing favorites, I understood the confusion in a house when one child is puffed up in an attempt to deflate another. There is a certain savagery in the abuse of family sovereignty.

Eventually, she lost interest in the game and set her attentions on achieving the escape velocity required to expel herself from the gravitational force of the family.

It was a long and complicated effort, but she managed her exit. I asked her about it decades later when we both worked to patch the holes in our relationship. She told me she was fleeing for her life, that she had to get out to save herself. Glen arguably dominated her. She wasn't allowed to drive or work or leave the house without an express purpose of meeting a need in her family. She was restricted to wearing blue or black, the colors of a bruise. Perhaps she was content wearing these colors as they matched her feelings. My memories of her inside 4766 Hurless Drive remain shadowy and ill-formed.

I remember seeing her laugh once. She was making pritzells with a hot iron she pressed into a batter and then into a deep pot of hot oil. The batter sizzled and flared out, conscribed to the delicate shape of the iron. She shook each pritzell loose of the iron and sprinkled it with confectionery sugar. She was playful in the sprinkling; it floated through the air with a frivolity the house was unaccustomed to. She was wearing a large black shirt with black slacks and when she noticed they were both dusted in the sugar, white patches of sweetness brightening such a somber backdrop, she laughed loudly, dropping her hand to her side, still gripping the iron wand. It was an uncomfortable sound, unfamiliar to both of us. We caught eyes and her mouth tightened quickly as she pressed the iron back into the batter, forming and conforming it in the hot oil.

It wasn't until many years later that Caroline walked out Glen's front door, the one reserved for guests who never came. It was cold out, that day in Ohio, as she turned the knob and stepped onto the front stoop without her coat. I remained silent as I watched her through the window. She moved down the long, tarred road framed between Tanner's two corn fields. She became smaller and smaller until I was unsure I could see her at all. I worried over her being cold, and considered, for a half a second, running after her with her coat. But by the time I glanced at the coat closet and back to her, she was gone. I turned away from the window to face the chill within.

While Antoinette and I both experienced suffering in our childhoods, her reflection differs from my own. With a casual dismissal, she accepts her family's favoritism of her sisters, her mom's drug and alcohol abuse, and her own sexual abuse under the watch of her grandmother and DSS. Addiction is a jealous partner, but to those living with a mother enthralled by alcohol and drugs to the exclusion of her small children, the addiction becomes selfish. Priscilla consistently chose men, drugs and escape over care for or belief in her children. And yet, while Antoinette speaks superficially of her mother, she is laudatory in her surface remarks, careful to protect Priscilla despite her years of abuse and cruelty. Priscilla continues to "parent" Antoinette with selfish focus, even with her daughter in prison.

"She blames me for Shaniya," Antoinette tells me one day on the phone.

Priscilla doesn't believe her daughter is guilty of the crimes that put her in prison but rather accuses her of allowing the crimes to occur by moving in with her drug-using sister, Brenda. I wonder if Priscilla is able to recognize the irony in her indictment of her daughter.

Antoinette speaks of a "mostly happy" childhood within a "close-knit" family culture. I see her childhood like I see my own, one marked by betrayal and pain. She admits to her mom's alcoholism and drug addiction to crack cocaine, but her memories blur around these defining traits to remember dolls and cousins and laughter. When the discussion turns to men in her mom's life, Antoinette becomes retrospective. She says she hated it when men came over. Antoinette considered herself her mom's protector. "I saw the way they treated her, beating her and this, that and the third," she tells me softly. "I hated her for not standing up for herself. I couldn't stand up for her, I was too little, but she should have been strong and fought for herself."

Antoinette remembers a consistent stream of men through their lives, which made her feel afraid. "I was very protective over my mother and couldn't stand nobody to touch her, couldn't stand nobody to look at her." She recalls her mom going back to her bedroom with different men when they came over. She learned to associate sex and drugs with abandonment. In this chaos and confusion, Antoinette would stand in the gap for her mother. Every man who walked down that hallway to her mother's room left Antoinette in charge of two young children, despite being a child herself. Every inhale her mother took from a pipe left Antoinette achingly alone and burdened by the needs of the baby and toddler who required care and supervision.

She says she would "go bang on the door and yell and kick and scream. I don't know, it's weird. I hated when men came around her because I felt they would take her away from me in some way, I guess. If that makes sense." She spent her childhood struggling to extract men from her mother's embrace to make room for herself. She could not know that even devoid of the men, her mother's arms could not protect her from the storms of this ocean. Poverty, drugs and despair swirled about her, causing waves of emptiness and hopelessness to crash against her little family ship.

Despite watching her mother beaten, abused, abandoned and used by the parade of men through the house, Antoinette grew up believing in happy endings. She recognized that the type of men seeking shelter from their own storms in her mother's care were not the men she wanted in her life. "I already had it in my mind, at that age, even though she didn't have good men in her life, in my mind I felt I knew what I wanted my good guy to be."

Antoinette's house was full of such instability, such chaos. Yet through her mom's alcoholic rages, she remembers the calm. She recounts watching the movie *Titanic* with her mom. Her voice is happy in the retelling. "I was a sucker for love movies, love stories, stuff like that." She laughs. She recalls *Titanic* becoming her favorite movie because it was the one she watched with her mom. "I was sitting there crying," she says with some emotion. "My mom said, 'I can't believe you are sitting there crying,' and I was like 'why can't you believe it?' You know what I'm saying, I was just CRYING." This is a happy memory for her, mother and daughter watching a movie together on the sofa. It is her version of my confectionery-sugar-flying-with-my-mom-laughing moment: an extracted memory, isolated and preserved as evidence of normalcy or happiness. But both Antoinette and I have manufactured such things. She may lack my cynicism, but we are both astute enough to recognize that one clear and hopeful memory cannot discredit a childhood of confusion and hopelessness. Our childhoods, like the *Titanic*, were not going to end well.

Appropriation

Antoinette went to school one morning; she thinks she was in the third grade. "I want to say Brenda was in kindergarten then." This hazy recollection is a recurring issue with Antoinette. She is blurry on memories and if asked to pin down specific times, even particular years, she backs away with an "I want to say it was . . ." This is challenging because it makes creating a reliable time-line based on her memories almost impossible. Her life was scattered about and it wasn't until November 2009 that her movements were pinned down to verifiable documents. From 6:52 a.m. on Monday, the 10th of November 2009 to Saturday, the 8th of May 2027, Antoinette's movements and behavior will all be documented as public record, but the twenty-eight years before that date are murkier. Her one memory that remains clear and sharp concerns an event that would tear her from her life with her mother. She is able to recall it with perfect clarity. It happened at Howard Elementary School when she was in the third grade.

Antoinette was called out of class by the school social worker and walked to a room where a Cumberland County DSS investigator sat waiting. The caseworker questioned her about life with her mom. Antoinette was too young to understand the implications of the questions presented to her by the DSS investigator, but her world would change based on her answers.

Antoinette laughed nervously when she talked about it. I could not determine if she felt guilty about what happened at her house after school that day or if she remembered how nervous she felt in that room. She said, "I told them what was going on. I mean, I didn't lie about what was going on." She either wouldn't or didn't tell me what she said that day to the investigator, but she had mentioned in previous conversations that her mother "was being abusive." When I pressed, she only said, "Yeah, verbally and stuff." Throughout all of our visits, letters and phone calls (totaling over eighty thousand words in transcription), Antoinette maintained this blurry distance from acute memory of her experiences with her mother. She backed away from any detailed account of her mother's actions. Antoinette was clear that her mother was addicted to alcohol and crack, but the effects of that addiction on her children were something Antoinette would not discuss.

Research suggests that Antoinette's life, as the oldest child of an addicted parent, was one of fear and conscribed responsibility. It would have fallen to Antoinette to tend to her younger sisters when her mother was behind closed doors with a man or behind closed eyes from the drugs. From her prison cell in Raleigh, she maintains a tenuous relationship with her mom now, but admits that even all these years later, her mom is incapable of participating in a relevant relationship with her. Back when Antoinette was a minor, DSS' involvement in her life suggests that Priscilla's abuse was severe enough to warrant the removal of three children from their birth mother.

I knew what it took for DSS to become involved. This same thing happened in my family, only I played Priscilla's role and it was my son, Jake, who was cordoned off in an empty room with a DSS caseworker at his school. Jake was questioned about his conditions in our home, and his views on my behavior as a mother. Like Antoinette, he was in the third grade. Specifically, the interviewer was looking for evidence of medical neglect or sexual abuse. I lived alone with my children; my Peter Pan ex-husband had long flown away from us by then. Jake suffered from a condition called encopresis, and, while it is medically rooted, it is attributed to emotional distress. It is a disturbing and complicated condition that results in the third grader being unable to control his rectal sphincter. Even if he was lucky enough to keep it contained, meaning it didn't drop out of his trousers onto the classroom carpet, he spent his early grade school years shrouded in the distinctive stink that is unmistakably attributed to defecation.

Like Priscilla and many mothers in poverty, I moved around a lot with my children, causing them to enter new school systems with alarming frequency. For Jake, this wasn't an entirely bad thing. He would pretty quickly garner the stinky boy reputation in every school he attended; and, with naïve optimism, I hoped each new enrollment would give him a fresh start. But it wasn't to be. This newest school was disquieted early on. His young teacher was fresh from a college graduation and her world held no such monstrous and appalling condition. This teacher's understandable aversion put into place a series of events that would alter our lives for the next year. When I came home from work the day Jake was interviewed without my knowledge or permission, I found a white business card from a caseworker—he was not yet *my* caseworker—tucked into my door jam. I read the card, which was surprisingly light on information considering the weight of its import. It read simply "Department of Child and Family Services." My heart flipped over in equal time to the card as I read the back, which revealed a handwritten "Thomas" with a phone number underneath. I fell to the floor outside our little apartment.

"Mommy, what's wrong?" The children pulled on me to get up.

I was paralyzed with fear. DSS was at my door and I felt instantly guilty without even knowing my crime. I looked to my children, hovering above me in the building's hallway. "What happened at school today?" I asked, scanning the row of six blue eyes housed in three innocent faces.

The girls shrugged with nothing to report and now the girls and I turned in unison to stare into Jake's steadfast gaze. "Some guy came to school and asked me a bunch of questions."

At this time, Jake was being considered for the gifted program and was frequently out of the class for testing. "Were you asked to take a test or something like that?" I asked hopefully. I had regained enough sense by now to get off the floor and get my little family inside.

"No, he mostly just asked questions about you."

I stared at the card, wishing ill-will toward the, now hated, "Thomas" that he could drop into my child's world, whisk him away without his mom or even a teacher present and drill him on issues well beyond Jake's experience or understanding. The children were all looking at me, gauging their response on mine. "I better give Mr. Thomas a call," I said evenly, and we all exhaled and went about our evening routine. It would be my last proper exhale for the next eleven months. I called Thomas on my break from work the next day. He advised me I was under investigation for medical neglect and sexual abuse against Jake.

The irony consumed me with a quiet rage. All those years of my own childhood, in every sense living under a man who needed a Thomas to leave a white business card on his threshold and *I* was the one under investigation. Justice, I have long suspected, is a belief held only by those who do not depend upon its tenets. The principal of Jake's new school made noisy proclamations regarding her frustration with what she saw as my lack of authority to solve Jake's condition. She had multiple choices that day; she could have called me to discuss Jake's treatment; she could have requested a release on his medical records or even contacted his therapist. She chose none of the above and instead, called DSS. That one phone call fell into my family's life with tremendous impact.

For the next eleven months, my house, my friends, my children and I were under a microscope of scrutiny, which produced an imaginary *guilty* bubble above my head. Thomas came to the house unannounced three times in those eleven months. He interviewed me on all three occasions, toured my little two-bedroom one-bath apartment, looked under all of the beds and, on one visit, even peeked in the refrigerator. I often wondered what he expected to find there. Baggies full of drugs? Were baggies of drugs even kept in the refrigerator? Shelves of beer bottles among the misplaced and lonely mustard bottle and grape jelly jar? Thomas interviewed my friends, my pastor, my boss, exposing

Jake's condition and my supposed culpability in that condition with no regard to the residue each interview left on the circling drain of my life.

Every day of that eleven months I worried that DSS would swoop in wearing riot gear and armed with court orders to extract Jake from our house and our lives. It was a terrifying time, each bedtime kiss goodnight held a sense of futility and was tainted with the fear of loss. The investigation exposed and invaded and in some ways, destroyed. One unremarkable day, it was over. Thomas was thoughtful enough to phone to inform me that the case was "officially closed." They are not required to do that. How many parents are currently gripping their children too tightly when they walk them to the school doors, wondering if today will be the day that they lose custody to the State, not knowing the case against them has been closed?

The DSS worker never considered informing all those intimate and peripheral people in our trespassed lives that he had found me "not guilty" and the charges "unfounded." For as long as we lived in that community, I felt both under suspicion and suspicious. Even all these years later, with Jake healthy as a young adult, I feel that sting of shame for even being associated in such an affair. I remain private and even reclusive as a byproduct of this one event.

It was a more devastating ending for Antoinette. Our family had survived the intrusion of DSS and remained intact. Antoinette's family, however, was pulled apart and altered irrevocably for the rest of her life. She said she didn't think anything about DSS the rest of the day at school. This made her surprised when she arrived home and found the DSS investigator in her living room. Antoinette remembers her mother "had said something that I had got so mad at her and I just started fussing and cussing at her—at this age—in front of the social worker. And I remember my mother saying, 'See, this is what I deal with, this is what I deal with. I take good care of them. You know I take good care of ya'll. Ya'll eat, ya'll go to school clean.' And I just remember after that, us leaving." The three girls were loaded into the investigator's car and taken to her grandmother's house. This was a homecoming for the sisters in that Priscilla had lived in this family neighborhood for their younger years before moving out to the apartment from which they were eventually rescued. I asked her what caused DSS to investigate in the first place. She said one of their neighbors in the Ramsey Street apartment complex had a falling out with her mom. "She had seen it all; she knew what my mom was doing." The girls would spend the rest of their childhood under their grandmother's care. "Our whole family lived back there in this little neighborhood. My uncles, my cousins, we all could just walk to each other's houses."

Her family homestead was off Ramsey Street, not far from her mom's apartment in the Fayetteville Housing Authority on Mary Street. Although her mom lived less than two miles away, she didn't see her "for a very long time." After some time had passed, whether it was a month or year Antoinette cannot recall, her mother started coming around again. "Yeah, she could never legally be around us period. But she still came around, and my grandmother never said anything. I guess that was because we needed our mother around, but my grandmother also knew how she was."

On the first occasion that Antoinette told me about her grandmother's custody, she seemed happy to have lived with her. But as our conversations began to pile up, she added details revealing a less ideal situation. What she originally cast as a tight little neighborhood of family, she later saw as more claustrophobic busyness around her. "My grandmother had nine children," she told me one day. "Nine."

I ask the gender ratio, and on this she is unsure.

"I want to say four boys and five girls." Because so many aunts and uncles lived next door, her grandmother's house was full of grown children who were jealous that their mother doted on her three grandchildren in a way that she had not doted on them. "My grandmother always had a house full of people; my uncles and aunts was always around. I hated it, I hated it. What made it so bad is that her kids would get jealous and say, 'Well, you're spoiling them; we didn't have a childhood like that.'" Antoinette tended to paint her childhood with broad strokes of happier colors. But she did admit, "We were torn up, and it was bad, real bad."

It's impossible to determine if the actions of DSS benefited Antoinette and her younger sisters. While it is clear that her mother's addictions and the consistent presence of strange men in the house could not produce a safe and thriving environment for the girls, it does not stand to reason that living with their grandmother, whose sons and daughters, according to Antoinette, used or sold drugs as a part of their daily patterns, would provide something more stable. DSS entered Antoinette's life a second time, this time with the spotlight aimed at her. The new investigation caused Antoinette to lose custody of her own children but, unlike her mom who had freedom to wander in and out of her grandmother's home, Antoinette never saw her children again. There was no snuggling on the sofa to watch *Titanic*. Her family ship had finally sunk.

The DSS Debacle

ALMOST A DECADE before Antoinette's child was taken by McNeill to be raped and murdered, and before her firstborn child, Carlesio, and her soon-to-be-born daughter, McKayla, were taken into foster care (McKayla was adopted shortly after her birth without the consent of her mother), Antoinette and her sisters were themselves jolted from their mother and placed into the arms of the State.

In 2009, the year Shaniya Davis was murdered, 379,000 children were under social service's care across the nation. Of those children, thousands were racially identified as black. Race was an implied issue during the media discussions surrounding the Shaniya Davis case. Her father, Brad Lockhart, appeared to be considered a white male of privilege and therefore beyond reproach, especially when pitted against her mother, a black welfare mom who was known as a sex worker and an occasional drug user. Shaniya's life seemed destined for the greatness of normalcy had she remained under her white father's dominion. All the trouble started, the press implied and the bloggers ranted, when that sweet little bi-racial angel was allowed access to her black whore of a mother. These were the popular opinions at the time. But Antoinette was more than that one statistic. Her childhood in foster care stacked the numbers against her long before she began dancing naked for Lockhart. While there is no current national study commissioned to examine such issues, three states (California, Illinois and Connecticut) initiated self-reporting surveys and concluded that 80% of their state's prison population once served time in foster care. Antoinette joined those statistics by walking into the prison system just shy of ten years after walking out of foster care.

In 1999, when the Davis girls were placed under a state-sanctioned guardian, the investigator was required to fill out an "Improper Care Worksheet" to determine the severity of intervention required. It asks questions such as "Is the parent providing sufficient food?" Antoinette assured me that "when my mom wasn't drugging, we always had a hot meal." She relays this information to me believing she is giving a good report. She means it as a loving testimony to her mother. Her younger years were informed by her mom's intoxication level. When her mom wasn't high or drunk, a hot meal was her mother's singular representation of a job well done.

Strangely, the DSS worksheet pays careful attention to the section on appropriate and reasonable clothing. DSS, as stated clearly on the checklist, does not care about name brands. This is actually written on the worksheet as, "Whether the clothing is new or name brand is not relevant to the discussion of whether the parent/caretaker is providing proper care; consideration is given to whether the clothing is sufficient to protect the child from the elements and health hazards." I take pause here to wonder why our social services division must make this disclaimer on the investigator's worksheet. Has the department been plagued by over-zealous neighbors calling to report a parent negligent because the kids weren't wearing Vineyard Vines? Nevertheless, the worksheet does include more pointed discussion.

It asks if the parent is gone for extended periods of time. This is a trickier one to define than if the child is wearing fashionable, name brand clothing. Does "gone for extended periods of time" mean a physical absence? Or can "gone" be slipped in as a pseudonym for "high" meaning "vacant" or "not present to parent?" The DSS manual does not make this distinction on the worksheet. But the worksheet does eventually address substance use. Its wording is cautious and shows an effort by the department to avoid judgment. "Are criminal elements endorsed by the parent that place the child's health or safety at risk?" It is worth noting that *endorsement* is not identical to *engagement*. The former word nods toward a shrug of "I'm not going to kick my friends out for lighting up a joint if the kids are in bed," while the latter indicts through inclusion.

Priscilla most assuredly endorsed *and* engaged in criminal activity that put her children's safety at risk. Antoinette's adult cousin molested her at family get-togethers from her sixth birthday through her ninth all under the anesthetized eye of her mother. "I had to see this man as I was growing up at family parties and cookouts. And there still are things that trigger me like certain smells. My mom never noticed. She was too busy drugging." Antoinette's life was an entanglement of drugs, social services and pain. This worksheet is one of hundreds like it found in the ninety-two-page Child Protective Services Manual.

Social work requires mountains of paperwork; this is an understood component of such a career.

When Shaniya Davis went missing, the Fayetteville Police Department's task force chief, Tom Bergamine, requested all existing files on the Davis household from DSS. They refused, making the task force wait three days for a judge's order. This refusal angered Cumberland County's District Attorney Ed Grannis, who threatened to charge DSS with obstruction, claiming the agency "dropped the ball" and that they appeared to be more interested in "protecting its image than protecting children." The North Carolina State Bureau of Investigation (SBI) launched a probe into the agency to determine its culpability by not turning over Antoinette Davis' records to the task force. The records they sought were not related to Antoinette's childhood but rather to her motherhood. Antoinette's uncle, Michael Davis, told reporters that DSS was investigating Antoinette's 7-year-old son Carlesio's safety in the house but said that DSS closed the case after finding insufficient cause to remove the boy.

But these claims, like many swirling around this case, cannot be substantiated. Whatever DSS did or didn't do, it remains only that Shaniya had more influence in their existence than they ever had in Shaniya's. In a press meeting, the director of Cumberland County Department of Social Services, Brenda Jackson, stated, "The Shaniya Davis case played a role in fostering reform at the department." She maintained a diplomatic silence toward her public aggressor, District Attorney Ed Grannis. The effects of DSS' actions were far-reaching.

In addition to the public shame the department endured during the investigation, Shaniya Davis' murder would also see the resignation of DSS' chairman of the board, Chet Oehme, who stated he was "ineffective in leadership" of the Social Services division. This is a shifty claim requiring the listener to determine if he meant that he attempted to assist the task force but those around him would not comply, or that, because of his decisions as leader, the task force was never able to receive the information they sought. Either cause results in the same effect. Oehme found a new position with Pennink & Huff Property Management but his performance evaluations don't fare much better there than they did at DSS. On a review page of his new company, one customer gave him one star, stating Oehme was "immature and unprofessional," while another reviewer added "childish" to his descriptors. So perhaps it is for the best that Oehme is no longer supervising the health and well-being of minors.

But Shaniya, of course, remains dead. All of this policy review and public outrage against DSS occurred, as it always does, far beyond the reach of the child it centered around.

I was at a bachelor party and he happened to be there and one thing led to another and we had sex. And after that, I gave him my number and he gave me his. I didn't call him, because I didn't think . . . he's a white guy, you know what I'm saying? He just wanted to be with a black woman.

He knew my feelings, but he just tossed me aside like I was nothing. I was just young and naïve, and I would do anything he'd ask me to do just so he would love me. You understand what I'm saying?

– Antoinette Davis

Pizza

I FIRST SAW him when I was in the sixth grade. He was with a couple of other boys who were pushing a piano down one of the hallways. We were the first class of sixth graders to attend school at Pfeiffer Middle School in Massillon, Ohio. It was a brand new building, and the classrooms were filled with the sharp chemical smell of new carpet and wet paint. That first sighting was early in the school year. I was walking through the expansive lobby, watching my reflection move ahead of me on the shiny, unscuffed floor, when I heard the boys laughing. I glanced up and saw Don Dekay. I was instantly and irrevocably smitten. The next two years of middle school were spent attempting to get him to glance back at me.

Despite a meritorious effort that tiptoed into obsessive territory, I was unsuccessful. Initially, I paid attention to his schedule and made a point to be nearby when his classes let out. This strategy required careful planning because he was on a "B" schedule that was housed a whole hallway away from my "A" schedule. I would dash out of my classroom at the bell, push my way through the huddles of popular and well-dressed pre-teens, and sprint across the connecting bridge to his hallway. Now I was sweating, both from the excursion and from the fear of getting caught. By this age I had learned to follow the rules in an attempt to remain unnoticed. But here I was panting to catch my breath, worried that I smelled bad from sweating, willing Don Dekay to notice me. He never did, or at least not in the way I intended. He certainly knew I was after him. I stuffed notes into his locker, wrote his name in long rows of tiny script across all my book covers and twice hyperventilated, falling to the floor, scattering my belongings and myself at his feet. But the more I fell toward him, the harder he pushed away. My Don Dekay saga became a pattern of performances, a pursuit of unavailable or overtly uninterested men into my adulthood.

When my firstborn started school, she was placed in Susan Hopkins' classroom. I did not like Hopkins with her small, cold smile masking her quiet disapproval of me. My escalating dislike of her throughout the school year was reciprocated; Hopkins' own animosity toward me increased to match my own. I wouldn't have been all that alarmed—after all, it was just one school year and my childhood had taught me to manage large quantities of pain for long lengths of time, but the school Allie attended was unusual in that the classroom teacher moved up with the students, meaning Susan Hopkins would teach Allie through her graduation almost a decade later.

At first, Susan Hopkins limited her antagonism to me. She would send home little notes about the lack of nutrition in Allie's lunch box or chide me for not bringing in colored pencils when it was my turn. Small things, really, but when the notes arrived with regularity, they began to feel like the report of a gun that held an endless supply of bullets. I was no innocent here and in no short supply of my own ammunition. I sent back a volley of piercing notes and made a point to pack Allie's lunches with bleached bread and generic fruit roll-ups, knowing my words and the food would gall Hopkins of the parental involvement and organic, whole foods philosophy. I packed Kellogg's Pop Tarts with an elfish delight, imagining the horror on Hopkins' face when the contraband was discovered.

We nipped at each other through most of Allie's first grade and found enough satisfaction in the game to stick with our roles. But by second grade, Hopkins began breaking the rules of engagement when she shifted the focus of her discontent onto Allie. Pressures grew as I involved the school administration in an attempt to reconcile and call a truce. Actually, this is partially true. I involved the administration with the end game of relieving Allie's distress at finding herself in the line of fire. But, I also found pleasure in exposing Hopkins' nefarious character to her peers and bosses. She was cunning and portrayed herself as an innocent victim of my ruthless tactics, but my campaign exposed her as the combat veteran that she was.

Near the end of second grade, the class was to perform a play, and Allie was given the part of the lead giraffe. Much excitement ensued. It was our first school event, and we solicited family members to travel in for the show. On the eve of the performance, Hopkins called our home and informed me that Allie was no longer the lead and would be put back into the chorus. The understudy would play the lead giraffe. I could hear the delight in her voice. I was gobsmacked on Allie's behalf. It was Hopkins' coup de grace.

For a variety of more complicated reasons, we left the school shortly after that, but for the next several years I allowed Hopkins to haunt me. I complained at every opportunity and attempted to cajole the mothers of Allie's classmates to join me in my growing rage. My closest friend in the bunch pulled me aside one day, likely wearied by my exhausting efforts to puff oxygen into a long extinguished firestorm. "If you can't make peace with this Susan Hopkins, another Susan Hopkins will show up in your life until you do." Despite being annoyingly svelte and wise, this particular friend was impossible to dislike. So I allowed her insight to settle within and even realized I had already been introduced to this lesson back in middle school, though in the case of Don Dekay, realization did not mean freedom.

Don Dekay continued to show up in my life through every man I chased but never truly caught. In fact, I made a point of choosing men I knew would never choose me back. There was the Don Dekay in college, a good-looking tennis star and upperclassman who held my hand on campus as bait to recatch his ex-girlfriend; the Don Dekay at the office, a brilliant attorney far above this humble receptionist; and there was even a bit of Don Dekay in my first husband, given that his homosexuality secured my quest for rejection. There was something about the doomed ending that energized my efforts. The more distant the possibility of being chosen, the more intense and consuming became my pursuit.

I managed a modicum of success in high school but this had more to do with my childhood inculcations of sexual strategy than with genuinely believing I was worth receiving true and honorable love. A few months into my junior year, I escaped my father Glen's house at 4766 Hurless Drive and secured housing for almost a full year by tramping around from friend's house to friend's house, continuing in my efforts to remain invisible. When one of their parents noticed me at the dinner table, I was asked, "Gosh, you've been here a week, don't you think your parents want you back home?" I could usually extend my stay by a couple of days by busying myself with household chores, overtly trying to become indispensable. Parents love that type of thing. This tactic would buy me enough time to convince another friend to let me spend the night.

But, once I ran through my intimate circle of friends, it became necessary to broaden my net and this is how I found myself staying at the houses of kids I didn't know very well. These houses were easier to stay in for longer periods because the parents were never around and when they were, they were too tired or drunk to notice me. There was little chance of being discovered at the dinner table because many of these families didn't eat there. Some of them didn't even have tables. The houses were dirty and usually lacked resources like laundry soap, food and, surprisingly, toilet paper. I began to steal rolls from public bathrooms and present them as an offering to my apathetic hosts. But as long as I remained helpful and cheerful toward the occupants, I was left alone.

It was in this particular circle of acquaintances that I was introduced to the dangerous and titillating world of high school parties. A ready supply of alcohol and kids I recognized from the vocational program made these parties enticing. The boys wore long ponytails and shadowed mustaches. They were always polite to me, bringing me a cup of Jack Daniels or scootching over on a sticky sofa to let me sit down. I felt a certain obligation to the boys to repay their gifts of attention and alcohol and courtesies with sexual favors. If I could grit through a high school boy's sexual fumblings, I might even snag a bed for the night. It didn't take long for my Sunday school sensibilities to soften watching all those boys' sexual sensibilities harden. It's a surprisingly quick plummet from sacred to slutty, and in the time it takes to recite the Lord's Prayer, I crossed over into the unholy land.

It was not uncommon for me to make out with several boys before ending up in a back bedroom with one of them on sheets stiff with filth, rhythmically attempting to be chosen. It was this pre-game warm-up that earned my nickname of "Pizza." When I was at a party, everybody got a piece. And so, when Antoinette told me about dancing at the bachelor's party and that one thing led to another when she and Lockhart had sex, I understood exactly what she was saying. It might have been three states above North Carolina and a decade earlier, but I had been to the same party. I was young and naïve and would do anything the latest incarnation of Don Dekay would ask me to, just so he would love me.

Shark

MARIO MCNEILL IS a bad man whom we readily and easily feel we understand within that context. Aside from the inconvenience of his intelligence, he fits the prescribed notions of what and whom we expect to be bad. He is black, he is poor, and he is a product of a single-parent household with multiple siblings. His crimes of pedophilia additionally service a preformed expectation of his life's performance: scary black man, hypersexualized, criminal. McNeill unwittingly adds to the stereotype of his species by selling drugs and growing dreadlocks. He not only offers a behavioral template for categorization but also provides a solid visual template as further evidence of his place in society. McNeill's criminality, in many ways, provides a reinforcement of traditional ideas that the dominant culture believes to be true.

While these traditional thinking patterns may work as a community net to identify and then isolate a particular type of person, predators who do not fit this profile are left to swim freely in the community ocean. We gather up the piranha only to leave the more innocuous but arguably more deadly sharks to feast unfettered.

Brad Lockhart was both great and white. Lockhart worked as a U.S. Army Civilian Contractor, a deliberately hazy title that identifies him as doing anything from the more benign Purchasing and Procurement to the more provocative Force Patrol. The Army rewarded him amply for his skills, and this bounty allowed him to live an upper middle-class lifestyle back home in Fayetteville, North Carolina. Little Shaniya was Lockhart's fifth child, and perhaps because he fathered so many before her, he did not celebrate her arrival.

Lockhart was unlucky as a father. Together with his first wife, Vickie Sue Coleman, he produced three children. For reasons that remain undocumented, the marriage crumbled, leaving Vickie Sue to raise the three children and Brad Lockhart to raise a ruckus with his reputation for parties spiced with crack cocaine and strippers. One evening after the divorce, perhaps out of boredom or old-fashioned loneliness, Vickie Sue picked up her younger sister, Chantel, from the hair salon for a girls' night out. They drove to an acquaintance's house nearby. There were three men already in the house, and the girls cozied up, perhaps smoking some of the wild stuff, when two men entered the residence with guns. They tied up all five of the inhabitants and ransacked the home. They were searching for a mythical lump of money, which was rumored to be hidden somewhere inside this "liquor house." One of occupants of the house had recently received an insurance settlement in the range of $100,000. Rumors circulating around the local pub indicated that the money was hidden somewhere inside the house.

So after the robbers tied up the five people, never mind that the two females were visitors in the home and one of them was an 18-year-old girl, they ransacked the house but were unsuccessful because, of course, the money was not hidden inside this crack house; it was safely deposited in the bank. But the thieves were either too dimwitted or too high to accept this. They began a protracted torture of the victims. One man was able to loosen his ties and hurl himself through the front window, an event that had cataclysmic repercussions. Once he broke through the window, the doped-up duo opened fire, catching him in the leg but not thwarting his escape. They turned their guns on the remaining four terrified people and emptied their weapons into the bodies. Despite the swarm of bullets flying from the execution squad, one of the men survived the attack, diminishing the murder count to three.

The loss suffered by Lockhart's father-in-law, Byron Coleman, was not diminished, however, in that two of the three people murdered called him "Dad." Vickie Sue and her little sister, Chantel, were pronounced dead at the scene, and the Coleman family, who had recently lost their young son when an aircraft engine malfunctioned, buried their two daughters just the way they had lived and died, side by side. The Colemans' distrust of Brad Lockhart became evident when they successfully sued for custody of the three grandkids. Apparently, Coleman long suspected his son-in-law, Lockhart, had something to do with the murders but nothing formally ever came from these suspicions. While it might not have been true for Antoinette Davis, speculation does not always lead to conviction. Vickie Sue's youngest girl would eventually wander away from her grandfather's house and into Lockhart's in the aimless way of teenagers, but it would be a short-term stay. He eventually kicked her out, causing her migration to the house of the neighbors, the Allens, where she remained until her emancipation. This child would be the only one of Lockhart's three children with Vickie Sue who would testify at McNeill's trial—for the prosecution. Although her life with Lockhart was splotchy and inconsistent, she developed a close relationship with her baby half-sister, Shaniya.

Before Shaniya was born, and not long after his children were tended to and raised by his former father-in-law, Lockhart exerted his human right, once again, to procreate. He sired a fourth child, but that relationship would never meaningfully scratch any kind of parental itch. The baby was forced to settle for court-required monthly child-support payments in lieu of actual contact. So, by the time Antoinette Davis was hired to dance at one of Brad's parties, Lockhart, despite fathering four children, lived as a bachelor.

When Lockhart met Antoinette at that first party, he was captivated by her looks. Davis is a tall woman, with creamy black skin and large, haunted eyes. He found her exotic and over the course of the next year, took her on as one of his possessions. There was the motorcycle, the speedboat and then there was Antoinette. Indeed, Lockhart called upon the skills he honed as a quasi U.S. Army operative by both purchasing and procuring Antoinette Davis. While there were never any police reports to validate the claim, it seems reasonable to assume he used his Force Patrol experience as well. Davis says, "I did everything he told me to do. If he told me to have sex with his roommate, I had sex with his roommate." She remained under his ownership for nearly a year before Lockhart's sperm connected with her egg with such enthusiastic determination that fertilization occurred. Davis, in her naïveté, believed she was in love with Lockhart and that this pregnancy was a harbinger of her promotion from employee to girlfriend, to, perhaps, even wife. Lockhart, arguably more experienced in such matters, quickly demystified the situation for her when viewing her outstretched hopeful hand. In place of a ring, he pressed her palm full of cash. "Abort this baby," he commanded as he dropped Antoinette back home on the other side of town.

Like many men in this desperate situation, he disappeared from her life for the next several months, perhaps to allow her time to recover and heal from her procedure. But Antoinette had ideas of her own. One of them was an indefatigable belief that abortion was wrong. "I'm not going to murder my baby," she told herself and anyone who would listen. She tucked the money away for the diapers and expenses of a newborn child and set her sights on a safe labor and delivery. Lockhart phoned her later in the year for a nostalgic booty call at which time he discovered that the breast he desired to suckle was already occupied by his daughter. He maintained an on-again-off-again sexual relationship with Antoinette during the next five years of Shaniya's life.

After Shaniya's death, Lockhart toured the nation's media outlets, crying salty tears over his lost child. He spoke of God and his unflappable faith. Although he later expressed forgiveness for Antoinette, he spoke initially of her unforgivable sins. He handily pointed to Davis as the root of the rotten mess, and the world nodded in a collective judgment. *How could that wicked woman do such a thing to this God-fearing white man?* the audiences may have thought as they watched his parade across *Oprah* and *Nancy Grace*.

The public gave no thought of Lockhart having culpability in Shaniya's death. McNeill was already locked up with the United States Postal Service clocking in over-time to deliver hate mail to his cell; Antoinette sat in her own cell, confined and childless, just how Lockhart apparently liked her. The police had already identified the villains in Shaniya's story, and they met the requirements of what we seek in bad guys. The piranha were hanging in the fishermen's net, and Lockhart slipped away within the dynamic current of public pity. The bad guys were caught and the ocean was safe to swim in once again. We prefer not to see *shark* when it is preceded by *great* and *white*. We prefer our villains to be black and dreadlocked.

Had Antoinette lived in a different set of circumstances, had her mother not been addicted to drugs and to the men who brought them, had DSS found a foster home even a few neighborhoods away from active drug activity, had the father of Antoinette's first child—the baby she birthed when she was just 16—provided financial and emotional support, had just one thing in her life helped her to step outside of the culture of poverty and hopelessness, the Shaniya Davis tragedy could not have happened. Antoinette would not have found herself as a 16-year-old, poor mother with no education or marketable skills. She would have had infinitely more choices of income rather than to strip for nouveau-rich boys in their cul de sac estates.

Antoinette wanted to give her daughter a chance to live and was willing to sacrifice even her own body to make Shaniya's life possible. Lockhart attempted to dishonor Davis when, in interviews, he called her a "stripping prostitute." But when seen in the context of her motivation, her sacrifice becomes noble. Antoinette was willing to dance naked for Lockhart and men like him to feed her hungry little boy, Carlesio, at home. What hunger was Lockhart feeding when he paid her, and others like her, to entertain and service him? Antoinette cannot be guilty of receiving his cash in exchange for her sex if Lockhart is not guilty of receiving her sex in exchange for his cash. It takes two hands to clap, and Lockhart paid for both of hers even while both of his were pointing fingers at her depravity.

Lockhart's lasting legacy to Shaniya's life is his abandonment of her on the steps of 1116A in the Sleepy Hollow Trailer Park. Granted, Antoinette pressed him for the child to live with her. A month later, when Mario McNeill kidnapped Shaniya, it took Davis less than one hour to call 911 in desperate fear. When Brad Lockhart—who stated he was going out of town, but also may not have wanted a small child interfering with his new relationship—dropped Shaniya off at the trailer park in October, he didn't see her again until his visit to the morgue in November. Both parents actively and with intention chose to place Shaniya in dangerous conditions. And yet the one who called for help, the one who risked everything to save her, is the only parent who lives in jail. Brad Lockhart remains free to "pray" among the rest of us.

Getting Off

I DISLIKED BRAD Lockhart long before I fully researched the details surrounding the crime. Like the general white population who feel they can sniff out a criminal based on a cursory head-to-toe glance, confident that hairstyle and shoe choices mark particular men as criminal, I am part of a general female population who feel we can pick out the libertine in the room. We rely on a more complicated rubric, but our assessments are just as cursory. Although these rakish men are not yet considered criminals in the formal sense, our quick judgment does not make those offended less wounded.

Lockhart exhibited a modicum of cleverness by choosing his victims among those already cast as villains. We want our courtrooms to convict those who offend our safety or morality, but we define these offenses based on the character of the one who is at the receiving end of the offense. Antoinette could hardly be considered a victim in Lockhart's life; she worked as a stripper by profession and was connected to drug users and pushers by neighborhood proximity. She was a welfare mom who dropped out of ninth grade to birth her illegitimate son. Lockhart was free to exploit, commodify, ravage, sell, use and possibly even rape Davis with impunity. Davis held no capital in the courtroom. I'm convinced that short of murder, Lockhart broke nearly every commandment issued under the God he wept to on national television. He coveted her, he lied to her, he stole from her, he blasphemed her, he idolized her, he dishonored her as a mother, and he betrayed her. But our current judicial system doesn't work well without a sympathetic victim. And so I believe Lockhart was permitted to socially get off even as he was salaciously getting off.

And So It Begins

APPROXIMATELY FIVE HOURS and thirty minutes before Antoinette Davis made her 911 call, a black Mitsubishi Galant turned into the Sleepy Hollow Trailer Park off Murchison Road. The driver, Mario McNeill, was a familiar guest in the park and known to several of the residents. For the past five years, McNeill was also well known to the Fayetteville Police Department. Two months after his 21st birthday, McNeill was arrested for his first felony. He was convicted of felonious assault with the intent to commit serious injury. For reasons undocumented, perhaps due to his young age or the fact that it was his first known offense, McNeill received a suspended sentence and was put on probation. Fast-forward two years and two months and McNeill is once again in front of a judge convicted with both possession and intent to sell a Schedule VI drug. This is a higher ranked drug, which typically refers to marijuana. North Carolina, like many states, categorizes its drug crimes based on a hierarchy that determines the addictiveness of a drug and its harmful side-effects. The lower the schedule ranking, the more serious and addictive the side-effects are considered. I tend to get very confused on this issue in that the "higher" number is actually the less dangerous drug. I feel like a first place spot should always go to the most deserving, in this case, meaning the least harmful. But drugs like methamphetamine and heroin are considered Schedule I, defining them as highly addictive and highly harmful.

Heroin and Other Addictions of Ministry

I KNEW A little something about heroin from my missionary days. Back when I was married to my now previous, Christian husband, who was trying very hard not to be gay, we served as missionaries to the poor in London, England. Initially, we were the supercharged members of an edgy group called Blood-n-Fire Ministries (BnF), based out of Atlanta, Georgia. The name was rooted in the motto from William Booth, founder of the Salvation Army, who ran it on his flag. But the leader of our little sect was closer to Jim Jones than the good general. David VanCronkite was captivating in an inclusive way, and he was also good-looking. These were two of his winning traits, but his real strength lay in his courage. He was ballsy, and my former husband and I were drawn to this fearlessness likely because we ourselves were so afraid. But before we smashed into each other's lives at a filthy downtown warehouse, VanCronkite, like many members of the Atlanta Vineyard Church, was a successful businessman.

This church was led by a former Mennonite, Johnny Crist, and his wife, Anne. Johnny Crist was a very good leader. His church attracted mostly middle-class

Christians who weren't scared of smart casual for their Sunday attire and stood unashamed as they swayed to the snare drum boldly added to their worship band. The Vineyard movement itself began its growth in California, tended to by a gaggle of former hippies who wanted to make church cool again. So they unrestricted the dress code and let suburban white folks clap their hands during songs that were no longer contained in stodgy hymnals but rather copied to transparencies and shown behind the pulpit on a sheet. Later, as both the church and technology became more sophisticated, the sheet was replaced by a slick super-screen and the handwritten transparencies by PowerPoint slides. The Vineyard Movement hoped to make Christianity sexy.

The vine grew eastward across the US through the late seventies and early eighties where it found fruitful soil in the hot suburbs of Atlanta. The Crists, an attractive young couple, tossed the biblical sensibilities of their Mennonite background with a pair of pressed blue jeans and a tambourine and suddenly the middle to upper class white-flighters found a home. Crist would later trade in his pastor's cap for politician when he made a successful run at Mayor of Lilburn, Georgia. But in the early days, the Crists tended to their growing flock of parishioners. They espoused some uncomfortable Charismatic Christian Movement leanings like speaking in tongues and falling out in the spirit, but, for the most part, the church made a successful jump from the old guard practice of serious study and terse whispered prayers to a feel good worship complete with flags and dancers and lengthy fevered prayers that required an "11:00 to ?" disclaimer printed in their programs. It was from this worship-centered service that the idea of serious missionary work was planted. There were only so many times one could repeat "Your life, Lord, not mine" in worship, without feeling a modicum of responsibility for the utterance. And so service to the poor became a focus of the growing church in Lilburn, Georgia.

And this was how David VanCronkite became invested in the outreach program. A small group of "yes" men formed around him as he drove a parade of SUVs down to the "inner-city poor" each Saturday. They packed their dark cars with groceries, first from the excess of their own pantries but later, as the interest and therefore the budget grew, from actual grocery stores. VanCronkite was wealthy, and this gave him some authority in the church, but his pretty teeth and even prettier eyes certainly helped secure his place as the definitive leader of the outreach. As much as the Christians sang and swayed about giving their lives away for the Lord, they had the sense to drive home from the worship service in air conditioned cars that drove into gated communities and parked themselves in warehouse-type garages that had room for two others just like it, or, twenty cots for the homeless, depending on the perspective.

The project to the inner-city became very fashionable outside the city's perimeter. Several more people joined in on the Saturday excursions. VanCronkite was even allowed to speak on Sunday mornings, cutting the worship time down, but nobody seemed to miss the extra song. And so it became a "thing." VanCronkite had scoped out an old, abandoned warehouse that sat in a strategic location. The Christians called it the Battlefield because they felt they were waging a spiritual battle. The city officials called it "the most dangerous mile" because the highest percentages of murders in Atlanta occurred within or around that city block. Fayetteville, North Carolina, holds its own distinction among dangerous cities in the state. According to *Neighborhood Scout*, a reporting service documenting crime statistics based on neighborhood, Fayetteville ranks four out of a possible one hundred on its crime index. This low score means that Fayetteville is considered safer than 4% of all the cities in the United States. Within its city limits, Fayetteville's statistics continue to portray a dismal picture of the neighborhood Shaniya Davis was growing up in. The Sleepy Hollow area did not make the top ten list of safest neighborhoods. Had VanCronkite's vision led him to Fayetteville, instead of Atlanta, he would set up headquarters on Murchinson Road within sight of the Davis sisters' trailer park. He would have seen it as the nerve center for crime, poverty and hopelessness.

But VanCronkite and his cronies marked their territory inside the Battlefield and they were hungry. They wanted more than the thrill of driving through the two housing projects that bordered that warehouse while tossing grocery bags out to the black children who ran after their cars. He was a visionary who cut his teeth in corporate America. He wanted to brand the city. And, perhaps, as some have speculated later, he wanted that real estate.

The church invested in a few industrial barbeque grills, and the little gang of fearless Christians set up shop in the parking lot of that oily, neglected warehouse. The warehouse—covered in city graffiti, displaying tiny rows of broken windows and with used needles littering the weedy parking lot—made the place look sinister and even violent. That was one of the appeals of the suburban folks who gathered there every Saturday night. It actually *was* sinister and violent. This scratchy patch of earth was not unique among poor neighborhoods. I felt that same dirty loneliness when duplicating the path McNeill took from Sleepy Hollow to the Comfort Inn in Sanford. Shaniya's last ride was visually punctuated by weedy cement parking lots leading up to storefronts covered in iron bars. Sad neon signs blinked in and out, adding the only color available to an otherwise gray and gritty landscape. Atlanta's urban poverty scenery looked much like Fayetteville's or that of any other city crowded with poor, unskilled people. This type of characterization inevitably conjures up images of bad guys lurking about the garbage-strewn parking lots and dusky alleyways. So it was for McNeill as well as VanCronkite and his merry band of followers.

The Christians clumped up against each other in that parking lot with their dry-clean-onlies and shiny sunglasses, hoping to shower the poor with barbeque from Jesus. VanCronkite's exploits became known outside the city's perimeter, and many churches of all denominations sent their most fearless types to serve the poor each Saturday. Courageous Christians trickled into the Battlefield in alarmingly small battalions, but what the churches lacked in courage, they made up for in tithes.

Whether it was the Vineyard's emphasis on worship music or VanCronkite's larger vision, a worship band was formed and soon the missionaries were lugging amps and microphones downtown, offering those living in the projects of Capital and Grady Homes both dinner and a show.

It was during this time that VanCronkite made a decision that, on its own, was a trifle. But when placed into a Nation Changing Narrative, became a major subplot. He dusted off his middle-age indulgence housed in one of the ports of his garage and began riding his black Harley Davidson into town. He stopped wearing shirts with collars in favor of t-shirts and ripped jeans. Perhaps most compelling, he wore a black leather jacket. It was only a few months later when they began printing the t-shirts. Stark white cotton with massive black letters with slogans like, "If you don't know Jesus, you don't know Jack" and, "Eternity, your choice: smoking or non." The new converts all sported the new Blood-n-Fire logo, and, during the worship concert, each member of the hungry horde received a t-shirt with his plate of barbequed chicken. The band wore black BnF t-shirts, and suddenly the most dangerous mile was looking more like a Club Med gone ghetto than the murder capital of the nation. It became an intersection of the impoverished and the privileged. The barbeque pits marked the territory that would later become the official cat hole, as it was lovingly called, for Blood-n-Fire ministries. A decade and some change later, VanCronkite would sell that prime real-estate for Georgia State University's new football field, using the proceeds to invest in, among other things, a fifty-eight-acre ranch in Burnsville, North Carolina, for just over a million dollars, or about two hundred thousand t-shirts, depending on the perspective.

But the interim years were spent serving the poor from this ramshackle lighthouse of love. Its beacon lit up my former husband's and my own squalid starter home, and with the enthusiasm of the ideal or possibly the desperate, we cast in our lot among the VanCronkite vanguard. We surveyed our service options and quickly became deflated. The band was the most alluring choice. They played pounding music and wore cool-looking black leather jackets. But we were not musically talented, nor were we even slightly cool. So, that left the barbeque line. These jobs were already taken by bearded, pot-bellied men who wore sleeveless t-shirts with sweat marks down the back as they flipped greasy chicken thighs over mammoth grills in the hot Southern sun. VanCronkite and his cadre of cul de sac colleagues parked their Harley's with prayer circle reverence and were busy in meetings held on the third floor of the warehouse. The only other service option available was to actually serve the poor. We had been taught to pray for them and we know how to feed and entertain them. What about housing them? Didn't we have a perfectly good basement in our little two-bed and one-bath home? We estimated we could fit six bunk beds down there, taking twelve people off the street. It wasn't a fully formed plan; we didn't have money to feed our own kids, for example, but we were zealots and believed that if we were obedient to the call of "going after the poor," God would work out the details.

Hunting

WE STARTED OUT boldly after church one night. We could have used a lesson or two from McNeill, who ran a modestly successful business of hunting for the hungry. VanCronkite held services every night of the week and required his volunteers to participate enthusiastically. We didn't yet have any beds in the basement; that would come a few weeks later, but we didn't bother with the details. Jesus had asked us to look after the poor, and week after week in those long worship sessions, we had raised our voices and arms in answer to the call. "Yes," we would give our lives away for the poor.

That first night, after a particularly unremarkable service, our family headed toward home in our jalopy of a car when our headlights lit up a man who was passed out on the sidewalk. We lived just a few neighborhoods outside the dangerous mile, and it was not uncommon to see street-sleepers among scary clusters of men who wore long jean shorts and even longer t-shirts. Many of them hid their wiry bodies inside those giant BnF t-shirts. The ministry had already successfully branded the mile. On this particular night, we drove up to a younger-looking street-sleeper. He was literally sleeping, lying partially in the street with his torso leaning up against a bus bench. We looked at each other and knew that we'd be taking him home.

This wasn't our first attempt. There had been one other man we almost took home a week before. He was lurking about the disintegrating warehouse parking lot after one of the services. It was high summer in Atlanta, and even at eight o'clock at night the broken-up cement radiated heat. I felt certain it was hot enough that I could bake a batch of cookies. This man was disoriented. He was rifling through the cars parked there, and, at the time, I assumed he was looking for a water bottle or some way to quench his thirst. Of course, that was back at the beginning when I believed they all were hungry for love and attention. I didn't understand the cravings for crack cocaine or heroin.

We offered the guy in the parking lot water, and the only reason we didn't offer him a place to sleep was because he smelled so badly from the sweat. Homelessness, I've learned, can be identified through scent. It puts off its own unique fetor of musty oil mingled with a stale greasy sweaty kind of stench. No matter how many gallons of bleach I scrubbed across our floors and bedding, I could never get that distinctive funk out of my house, out of my hair. But this first man was especially rank, likely because he had a long raggedy beard that swelled across his ample stomach. So, because it was our first time to invite someone home, we were unsure and easily allowed our uncertainty to dictate our actions. We left him with the water bottle and went home without our first guest.

But this night was different. Firstly, this second man had no beard, which moderately disarmed me. But the weather shone its favor as well by providing a thunderous storm. It was the kind you watch from windows or doorways because the rain is so heavy and in such high quantity you feel you are standing behind a massive waterfall. And here was this young black man, just leaning against the bus bench. He wasn't sitting on it, possibly because he lacked the strength to move himself up to it, but rather leaned against it, a picture of hopelessness, which was the very thing we were searching for. I knew it was inevitable; we were going to open our home to the homeless, and this moment seemed like the right person at the right time. I wasn't so much distressed about getting him out of the rain as much as I was relieved that, because of the rain, he wouldn't smell so badly.

Jeff Batton got out of the driver's side and ran to his aid. I surveyed the back seat, wondering where we would put him. Our three small children were all strapped in, staring out the window at their dad who appeared to be playing the part of an umbrella as he leaned over the man slumped against the bench. I made a mental decision to squeeze myself between two of the car seats and put the man in the front when my husband knocked on my window. The rain fell so hard it bounced off his shoulders and the top of his head. I stared at him in one of those eternal moments, a light from a restaurant sign lighting up his thin frame from behind, illuminating the drops of water hitting his body and repelling off with force and speed. I didn't know it at the time, but this was a life-changing moment—Jeff standing there drenched by the summer storm, knocking on the window of our sad, cheap little car, asking us to accommodate a stranger he found in the street. I flashed back to his image outside my car window that night during the desert years that followed, wondering what would have happened had

I not opened my door. At the time, it all seemed so pressing, so urgent. We were taught to "go after the poor" and it felt righteous and life-giving. But distance offers perspective and I now see those years as more of a hunter going after its prey.

We went after the poor to satisfy a hunger inside of ourselves. We espoused, and even for a time believed that our actions, our sacrifice, our nobility was for those we hunted. But it was a masked benevolence. All those years of giving up beds and splitting an orange twelve ways for breakfast, those sacrifices were always for us.

At first the poor represented a lack, a deficiency that we felt we could diminish with bold actions of love. The more radical, the better the sound byte on Sunday morning. I watched Jeff literally remove his shirt to hand it to a crack addict over twenty times. He once gave his treasured jacket, a parting gift from his dying mother, to a man who was HIV positive. I watched this emaciated man fight, with the last dying moments of his life, to wrest himself from one of our basement bunk beds, tuck Jeff's jacket under his frail arm and walk weakly toward the nearest dealer in search of a trade, one beloved jacket for one last rock in his pipe. Three days later, Jeff found him in a well-known cat hole a few doors down from the warehouse. He was dead, still wearing the new white socks we had bought him a few days before. The jacket, of course, was draped across another addict's shoulders as a mantle around an ox.

These grand gestures could not have been for the benefit of the poor. We were decidedly not benefiting the poor. We became willing martyrs in the name of Blood-n-Fire. We were the darlings of the warehouse because our radical stories translated into rich tithes from suburban churches.

But on this rainy night, Jeff Batton stood illuminated in the car window, and I couldn't know the consequences of opening that door. He was out of breath. "I need your help getting him into the car," he said as he glanced back to the man, who hadn't moved through the entire encounter.

"Can he not walk?" I asked, not wanting to become so physically involved. I didn't want to touch him. But my husband was slight and unable to manage alone, so I dove into the rainstorm with him and together we carried the homeless man to the passenger seat. I snuggled in between two of the car seats in the back, and we drove toward home. I don't remember the girls saying anything about this bizarre decision, and it would happen so many times after this night, that it is unlikely they saw it as odd when placed in the context of their young memories.

Beggar, Beggar

THIS ONE RAINY night would shape the course of our next seven years. My children would grow up in houses full of the homeless. They would watch as I made pallets on my bedroom floor for them so their beds could be used for the especially sick who would require attention through the night. It did not escape my notice that Shaniya was sleeping on her aunt's sofa the night danger was invited in. I consider her tiny frame, sleeping on a dirty sofa when McNeill's shadow darkens her. My own children slept on sofas with many shadows darkening them. I don't know how many dangerous men or women we invited into our home during this chaotic frenzy of service, but I can state with unequivocal certainty that any of the unknown guests could have been a McNeill.

My children would watch as many of their belongings were used or stolen, including my son's tricycle, which we later found discarded outside Dusty's BBQ inside the dangerous mile. It remained intact but for one of the tassels that hung down from the shiny red hand grip. I always thought it strange that only one side was torn out. What did they use the tassel for and why would they only need one?

We chose to "give our lives away for the poor" and in doing so, pressed our three children into a form of indentured service. Serving the Poor was their family business and they were expected to sacrifice for it, even at the cost of their innocence.

That first rainy night, the children and I stared at the back of the man's dripping head. He remained in the position we had settled him into, and I began to wonder that he was dead. I watched him intently for signs of life—a twitch, a shoulder shrug—but the only movements on his person were those of the water dripping from his short hair into little puddles on the seam of his shoulder before running down his arms until the trails evaporated from the tepid air pushing out from the car vent. I began to worry about illegally transporting a dead man, thinking it would be just like us to jump into sacrificial living only to load a corpse into our family car and take him home for dinner. But as we pulled into our driveway, I was relieved when the man showed definitive signs of life by succumbing to a coughing spasm that immediately sent me off to worry over tuberculosis. It was later determined that he was infected with pneumonia. At the time, I found his diagnosis relieving, but now I see things from the perspective of *mother*, not *missionary*. I now wonder about my children that night. They lay in their little beds, all lined up like orphans in the second bedroom while this stranger, who was now wearing one of their dad's shirts, coughed and hacked through the long night from his resting place in the center of our living room.

In the morning, we worked around him, sleeping there on the sofa, keeping to our regular schedule of tea and breakfast. He finally woke up when one of the girls tossed a ball off his chest. He sat up confused and commenced a memorably long coughing jag. When he quieted down, I asked him if he wanted some tea. He declined and said he needed to get back to Grady Homes, the housing project that bordered the back of the warehouse. He was too weak to move from the sofa and ended up stranded there for almost three days. But like Jesus from the grave, he arose that third day and walked out the front door, his addiction to crack serving as a compass from our house back to his supplier. He was very weak and walked slowly, but he held a determination in his face that I was not prepared for. Like the prophet Isaiah, his face was set like flint.

It was all very anticlimactic. For the first day and, into a portion of the second of his time with us, Jeff and I tucked in his blanket and fussed over him like a sleeping puppy in a box. I offered him food and drink. He always declined the former but eventually accepted the latter. But after a while, the tasks felt like tending to one of the girl's baby dolls. He was non-responsive and too sick to feel any kind of gratitude for our sacrifice. That is how it felt later. But at the time, we were still hooked on the BnF Kool-Aid. We weren't looking for gratitude but rather for ways to selflessly serve the poor. But even Jeff, who was the most ferocious Christian I would ever meet, found the service itself quite dull. He was already tracking down bunk beds for the basement, thinking that what the experience lacked in quality, he could compensate in quantity.

And so it came to pass that we would stuff twelve men in our basement and win them to Jesus through acts of love. We officially turned our home into a flophouse. Many of the men were too high to remember their stay in our basement, the morning rounds of

Styrofoam coffee cups delivered to their bunks, the big-pot meals of whatever we could get from the BnF food pantry for supper, the kids underfoot, the lines for the bathroom with the Little Mermaid sheet hanging where the door was meant to be. And I don't remember them either, not singularly. But, when I think back on these years, I see an endless collection of homeless men stretching from our house all the way back to the BnF warehouse. When I allow for the memories of our time served in London and Hong Kong, the line expands to one long desperate assembly of hopelessness shuffling across the whole of the globe. Our personal equator of inequities.

Because we had lived with the poor, we became very knowledgeable in some of the common traits shared among the misfortunate. Actually, it's not so much that we *lived with the poor*, that makes it sound noble or that our choices held a glorious meaning. The truth of the matter is that we *were* the poor. We begged from wealthy church members *in the name of the poor*, but perspective provides an ability to recognize irony. Every time we spoke at a church, or enjoyed a fancy dinner to offer us "restoration" for our service, I would secretly will our benefactors to stash money in our pockets or fill grocery bags from their pantries to stock my own barren one.

We became an unnecessary middleman. Had we gone to work ourselves, earning actual cash instead of accolades, we could have served the poor directly. But by forsaking the work place, leaving "the world" as it was commonly referred to in the Blood-n-Fire circle, we became the very beggars we hoped to serve. Our begging was more sophisticated than sitting on a pitch with a cup, yes, but it was no different. Or perhaps it was different in one defining way: the truly impoverished begged with authenticity; as missionary Christians, we begged with hypocrisy.

Despite our motives, we did learn about street sleepers and addiction. Crack, particularly in Atlanta, prevailed as the prom queen of street drugs. We once had a family living with us in our partially converted attic. The parents were crack addicts and used their combined monthly welfare allowance to check the family into a hotel for three or four days. During this family holiday, the mom and dad converted the remaining amount of money into rocks of crack. They came back to our house looking exhausted. When discussing his parents' monthly binge, their boy, Jamal, complained to me once, "That crack smoke give me a headache."

That crack smoke was invasive. Although I never smelled it personally, I felt its effects on those living with us. It clung to them like a disease swirling around the community. Antoinette knew this smell well throughout her childhood. Like Jamal, Antoinette lived in a house that was frequently full of the smoke that produced erratic behavior in her mother and would leave Antoinette with headaches. The family who lived in our attic operated under a belief that their behavior and choices were "normal." The children, often homeless, always hungry, would grow to fear the monthly support checks as much as they yearned for them. Each month they knew that the money would buy them treats and a proper bed for a few days, but they also knew that those provisions came at the cost of the drug smoked through their parent's pipe. Antoinette's childhood held a distinction only in that the frequency of the drugs was not connected to a monthly support check. Antoinette grew to fear her mother's drugged conduct every time a man walked through her front door. The night Shaniya was kidnapped, a man with drugs walked through her front door.

When we "served" in London, I became good friends with a heroin addict named Sally. She was elegant, almost regal as she sat on her pitch, begging for money by McDonalds. She had a prime pitch location in that the tourists were drawn to McDonalds, confused by the local restaurant choices of mushy peas and blood pudding.

Every once in a while she would end up in the hospital for some complication with her addiction. She had an ice-cream-scoop sized divot in her right thigh, a common sight among heroin addicts. She must have missed a vein one night and pushed the poison into her flesh, rotting it away. And it was no wonder she missed her vein in light of the conditions she endured for that drug. The heroin addicts in that neighborhood shot up behind the Mother Care shop just off the high street in Brixton.

There was an alley behind there that looked so iconically "druggish" that I sometimes wondered if I was on a movie set. It smelled of urine and always had one or two people leaning up against the back of the shop high or just about to be. I found Sally back there one time and she admonished me, "I don't want you seeing me like this," although I saw very little difference in her demeanor from the way she behaved in the front of the shop. She was vacant in both places. The missing piece of her flesh acted as a metaphor for the missing piece of her humanity. The drug had carved both out of her body.

I always liked it when she was in the hospital because she got to lie in a bed with a pillow. For almost a year I invited her home with me, unsuccessfully luring her with images of bubble baths and hot tea poured into a porcelain cup; but she never came. Once, lying in a hospital bed, her bony face pale and thin, she whispered, "Heroin. Now heroin I have to have, but crack, that is just for pleasure." Within the year, Sally died on that pitch.

Later, in that same year, a young feisty girl named Gemma, who worked as a prostitute to maintain her addiction, came to dinner at our house high on heroin. We all sat around the table singing our prayer, "For health and strength and daily food, we give thee thanks, oh Lord" and before we could finish with a somber "amen," Gemma's head collapsed into her plate of spaghetti, where it would have remained for some time, had the shock of such actions not worn off so long ago. One of us gently lifted her head from her plate, cleaned her off and escorted her to a bed.

So I understood these Type I and II drug classifications and while I mostly tended to those who were at the using end of the drug, Jeff went in search of those who were at the pushing end. I now believe that our chaotic and risky lifestyle was a form of addiction in itself. We experienced a certain "high" in answering our door in the early hours of the morning, preparing a pallet for one of the children so the sick or desperate could have a bed. We became addicted to the power of feeling needed. The poor became personal. We sought after them in the streets, injecting them into the veins of our home with as much focus and intent as I have seen among even the most desperate drug addicts. The ministry became our supplier and our drug was available in abundance. The cost, of course, like all addictions, would be paid for by the next generation. Our children would carry the burden of the sacrifices we made in the name of our personal savior.

I'm certain many, possibly hundreds, of drug deals were transacted in our very living room as user and pusher crossed paths on the way to the bathroom. And so I had met many Mario McNeill's with their long hair and confident swagger. I knew them to lurk under the cover of a deep night. I was not surprised to hear Barbara Davenport, proprietor of the Sleepy Hollow Trailer Park from where Shaniya Davis was kidnapped, testify in court that McNeill's black Mitsubishi lurked into the park at twenty minutes past two in the morning. This was the beginning of his business day.

Two Big Dogs and Two Little Children

BY ALL ACCOUNTS, McNeill did not behave strangely or in any way outside of his routine all day Monday, November 9, 2009. Early that night, he spent time with his girlfriend, April Autrey, at her house where she lived with their two small children. It is unclear how long the two had been dating, but McNeill had ended a previous relationship with Antoinette's little sister, Brenda, just a few weeks before, so it is reasonable to assume the relationship between McNeill and Autrey was an open one. McNeill felt close enough to Autrey to move into her place, bringing with him two very large dogs. Much fuss would be made later over those dogs, with multiple pictures of them submitted into State's evidence. But on that Monday, the dogs and children spent their day happily within their expected habits. That night the children were put down to bed, the dogs were let out for their evening constitutional, and the little house on Pine Springs Drive was closed up for the night. All would have ended happily ever after had McNeill chosen to spend the remaining hours of that night at home. But McNeill felt like prowling. At 2:15 on that cold, rainy Tuesday morning, he left Autrey's house for Sleepy Hollow Trailer Park, about a sixteen-minute drive. His cell phone would not ping back to Autrey's location until almost nine o'clock the next morning. It's difficult to imagine him leaving home that night. Sometime before 2:15, as he testified at his murder trial, he got high on cocaine. At some point in the night, he may have peeked in on the two children sleeping there. At two in the morning, most children are dreaming safely. Shaniya certainly was.

Somehow, McNeill managed to tiptoe away from these two children only to kidnap and rape a third child less than three hours later. By eight o'clock that morning, just one hour before he would return to Autrey's house, he would murder Shaniya Davis by placing his hands over her mouth and nose until she struggled against him no longer. Those same hands would arrive home within the hour to pour cereal into bowls for the children whom he let live that night.

38 Minutes

McNeill's next movements are a subject of much speculation. Jason Sondergaard, a Fayetteville police officer, testified at the murder trial that McNeill made over thirty calls during this time before approaching 1116A, Shaniya Davis' home at 2:58. That's nearly one call a minute. I considered that most of these calls were to his customers and became impressed by his focus. I had a sales job in Atlanta. The quirky South African owner of a boutique potato chip manufacturer called PotatoFinger took me in after my divorce, much as I had once taken in the lost and hopeless. He hired me, and later my twin sister, to be his Chip Girls, selling his boutique chips wholesale to local restaurants and corner grocery shops. Even with a cold call list of thirty shops to solicit within one hour, I could not have accomplished what McNeill did in half the time. I'd call one or two, then get up for a bathroom break. A few more calls down the list and it would be time to steep a nice cup of tea. Steeping tea, when done properly, can take up to six minutes. I pictured McNeill sitting in the car he borrowed from his girlfriend, calling thirty numbers within thirty-eight minutes and knew he would handily be named salesperson of the week.

Added to his business acumen is the fact that some of McNeill's calls were social, meaning they clocked in at more minutes than his business calls. I estimated his professional calls were likely placed in under a minute. After all, how long can it take to say thirty times, "I've got your drugs"?

There was no dispute that McNeill was a drug dealer and that he successfully serviced many of the residents of Sleepy Hollow. When questioned by police, both the dealer and the dealt admitted to their professional relationship. In McNeill's trial, District Attorney William West chose only one Sleepy Hollow customer to represent the whole neighborhood much like an attorney does in a class-action suit. They choose the most sympathetic representation to highlight the outrageousness of the offense. Tasia McLain became the prosecution's delineation for the whole of the Sleepy Hollow territory that McNeill claimed as his own. She was an astute choice because she not only placed McNeill into the role of drug dealer, always a positive thing if you are a prosecutor, but she also placed McNeill into a timeline that definitively put him into Shaniya's house by 2:58 a.m. Her testimony corroborated the video surveillance of the Sleepy Hollow Trailer Park, which shows McNeill leaving Tasia's trailer at 1119 Sleepy Hollow Lane and walking across the scratchy, brown earth to her neighbor's trailer at 1116A, where the little 5-year-old girl lay fast asleep.

Tasia McLain testified for eighteen pages of the court transcript about scheduling a date with McNeill that night. He was supposed to come over "for cards and drinks," but she had fallen asleep by the time he was seen knocking on her door at 2:57 that early morning. It's hard to know if the night would have unfolded differently if she had answered his knock. If Tasia had invited him inside and fixed him some drinks while they sat and "played cards," would his hunger have been satisfied? Would Antoinette have awakened for work that morning with her daughter nestled in safely next to her? Perhaps Shaniya would have played with her beloved Barbie doll while she ate her breakfast cereal that morning. If McNeill had not spent those thirty-eight minutes making phone calls from his girlfriend's car, Tasia may have been awake to welcome him in and Shaniya's Barbie would have remained where it belonged, in her innocent little hand, rather than where it ended up as a permanent decoration on her tombstone.

Suburban Sanctuary

When I began my research for this story, I wanted to physically take the geographic route Shaniya took on the dark morning of November 10, 2009. So, I dragged my husband, Simeon, over to Fayetteville from our hometown of Asheville and gave him the task of driving through Fayetteville and photographing each site. His ancillary jobs included fixing my tea just the way I like, waiting sometimes hours in the car while I interviewed people, and kissing me when I felt discouraged. There would be much kissing on this first trip.

Before Simeon, like Antoinette, I had very bad luck with men. And even Simeon caused me a profound amount of pain before we found our happily ever after. Like me, Antoinette set her sights on the good guys like Jack from *Titanic*. Unfortunately, like me as well, she ended up with guys who "only wanted to party." My first husband, Jeff, didn't want to party in the way that Antoinette meant it, but we had our own destructive version of partying in our focused devotion to the Church. There was a recklessness in the way we abandoned everything for the high we got from radical service to the poor. Antoinette's guys partied in the more traditional ways, slouching on her sofa, filling their bodies with alcohol and drugs. My living room sofa held slouching men who very easily could have come from her house the day before. We prayed and worshiped all around them, served them dinner and tucked them in. This left them rested and refreshed to hunt down the next woman's sofa with promises of love and devotion on their lips, but with a pipe and a rock of crack in their pockets. And so it went for years and years, Antoinette searching for love in the lost, and me searching for the lost because I was in love. When the BnF party ended seven years later, I slept on my girlfriend's sofa with the children on pallets around me where we were tucked in and tended to until we were strong enough, refreshed enough, to move forward. Antoinette was offered no such respite. Ever hopeful, perhaps even a bit naïve, she continued to open her door to her family and her family's friends, thinking one of them might become her happy ever after. One day her door would be opened to her sister's friend, Mario McNeill.

After BnF and my first marriage, I worked for Starbucks, making $8.20 an hour. Like Antoinette, I was an unskilled laborer whose only real talent lay in personal hospitality. We both knew how to please other people at our own expense and sacrifice. But I had an advantage over her, my friends had either had some college credits or had earned their bachelor's degrees. They watched me arrive at work at 5:30 in the morning, leaving my 10-year-old to get her siblings ready for school and onto the bus. They encouraged me to go back to college. Beyond that, they actually believed I could go back. Things were markedly different with Antoinette. No one in her world, her neighborhood, her living room, had gone to college or had the energy or ability to see past the poverty and despair. She herself had left school in ninth grade because she was pregnant by her live-in boyfriend who moved out about the same time her infant son moved in. My friends offered me a way out of poverty. The only escape Antoinette was offered was through the drugs she had watched destroy her mother and grip her youngest sister. It was a life she rejected because she knew this life to hold emptiness. While she admitted to smoking pot, she forcefully told me that she would never do "illegal" drugs.

Like me, Antoinette received no child support for her two children from their fathers. My friends helped me negotiate the discouraging and daunting world of Child Support Enforcement. There I was able, after six years of effort, to have my former husband's salary garnished. In those long, dry years without the support, we lived on my minimum wages and consistent and generous support from my girlfriends. Their support came in all manner of ways. They offered financial support, food and babysitting, and when I had a tough exam, they even cleaned my house on countless occasions. My life was filled with givers, girlfriends who stitched patches into my worn and holey life. Antoinette's life was filled with takers who stretched her scarcity thinner and thinner, offering her no assistance or encouragement.

I did go back to college, earning my bachelor's degree, surrounded by a network of people who helped me achieve my education. Without my little group of girlfriends around me, making pots of soup for children, helping me make my rent payments, I would not have made it to graduation. I often think about Antoinette, with her quiet intelligence. Had her circumstances been different, had she any modicum of fellowship or even one person in her life who could offer support without a demand for some sort of payment, she and I could have walked across the graduation platform as peers. Antoinette and I could not dream largely for ourselves; we did not find ourselves worthy of self-hope. My friends dared to dream for me. This support in my life is what lengthened the distance between Antoinette's outcomes and my own.

After graduating from Georgia State University, I felt strong enough, healed enough, from my divorce and suffocating church experience to consider a master's degree. Like Antoinette's decision to move into the Sleepy Hollow Trailer Park with her sister, my decision would alter my life irrevocably.

I made it to grad school and, like most students, spent most of my time in the library. One day I was headed to the coffee bar that was housed inside the library when I first saw Simeon. He was sitting on the sofa with the scratchy cover, his long legs crossed with his ankle resting on his knee. He was reading a paper he held in his, what I thought to be, elegant hands. He was biting his full bottom lip with his top teeth. I was on my way to get a hot chocolate before my grad school class that night. I had to walk past him to get in the line, and I was absorbed by him, so taken by his presence that I openly stared as I walked to the café. He must have felt the intensity of my gaze because he looked up from his paper. I kept walking and watched him as he looked down to my hand, which was carrying a heavy fan. My boss in the writing center where I worked on campus told me I could have it because the center no longer needed it. But it was a big fan, round and heavy, and its size made my walk clumsy and limpish. It was this fan that Simeon stared at while I stared at him. I turned my back on him to order my hot chocolate and by the time I turned around to him, licking the whipped cream from the top of my cup, he was smiling. And that was it.

Every minute forward from that moment ticked by with a new reality. I was in love.

This was a very surprising condition for me. After that long marriage to a man who first married the Church and then, ultimately, married the gay lifestyle, I felt cynical toward love. I married Jeff Batton because I felt it was the right thing to do. I certainly never needed a man. But now here was Simeon with his intellect and his loping walk and this chewing on his alluring lips and I was undone. I wanted him. I wanted Simeon more than I wanted anything before, more than my education, more than my desire to escape poverty, more than even my sacred twinship.

And so it began. Simeon disrupted my delicate but determined approach to life. I had been divorced seven years by now, and in all that time I had never felt lonely or lacking without a man. I had felt just the opposite: I felt freedom. Now I was in love, the kind I watched at the movies, the kind that made my heart beat funny, like a flutter of panic and wave of euphoria at the same time.

Many years ago, my twin sister and I had the misfortune of having the back end of our old clunker of a car smashed into by a driver who didn't see us stopped at the red light. Rather than fix the damage, we decided to take the insurance money and run toward fun. We ended up on a snorkeling tour in Hawaii. We put on those tight masks and stuck the rubber pieces into our mouths, ready to jump off the boat for our adventure. The island had experienced some unusual storms the week before we arrived, and so the water was unexpectedly cold. We jumped off that sunny boat into that deep, frigid water, and the shock of it against our hot, sunburned skin was jolting.

Suddenly, I couldn't catch my breath and started to panic. Just as I was thrashing about, the water cleared and I saw the bright colors of the coral reef through my mask. I had never seen anything like it, even in pictures. It was a world unknown to me. I was instantly calmed and intrigued even while my skin was still adjusting to the cold. I was moved by a school of tiny fish all swimming together like a cheerleading squad with the sun filtering down in slanted, wavy lines against their pink backs. I was enthralled and captivated even while fighting off a panic attack at the cold, heavy water. This was what loving Simeon felt like to me. A constant struggle between enchantment and panic.

After two years of a courtship complicated with my neurotic angst and his reluctance to end a lukewarm but safe relationship he was in when we met that day in the library, we finally sank into the fascinating bottom of our own ocean, navigating the sharks together. We were married for two years when I felt drawn to Antoinette and her story, which brought us to Fayetteville on that first research trip.

Our first stop was in the upper middle-class neighborhood off Elliot Farm Road in the Longleaf subdivision in Fayetteville, North Carolina. The white brick, traditional home at 7935 Lester Drive cost a little over $100 a square foot, and this spacious house had 2,419 of them. This was the home of Brad Lockhart, Shaniya Davis' father.

Shaniya had been living with her mother just under a month at the time of her abduction because she had lived full-time with Lockhart, or one of Lockhart's girlfriends, up until October of 2009. So, the majority of her first five years of life were spent inside 7935 Lester

Drive. She lived in comfortable luxury at his home with a manicured lawn and a double car garage. At the time of my investigation, Lockhart had long since moved to the western United States with his girlfriend, Lisa Maria. During the kidnapping and then later, at the trials, the media outlets speculated that it was Lockhart's relationship with this girlfriend that had caused him to drop the child off at Sleepy Hollow Trailer Park to live with her mother. But there was much more to Lockhart than the round-faced, weeping man seen on televisions around the nation.

We arrived at his former neighborhood to find a quiet, uniformed row of houses sitting on third-of-an-acre lots off curbed streets. Lockhart's house, like all those around it, sat on a pretty green lawn off streets with names like Banker's Court and Splurge Drive. There was a carpet cleaning van with a sign boasting a

BRIGHTER IMAGE

parked on the street opposite the former Lockhart residence, making it a clean jump in the brain to guess that the order and tidiness seen on the outside of the homes would be replicated on the inside. Shaniya left this life of middle-class, white privilege about five months after her fifth birthday party. Early in October of 2009, Lockhart buckled Shaniya into his SUV and drove her from this spacious neighborhood to the trailer park at Sleepy Hollow. The drive would take him eighteen minutes, about the same amount of distance her kidnapper and murderer would travel from his own little stand-alone home to the steps of 1116A Sleepy Hollow Drive just a few weeks later.

Brown

We followed McNeill's route now, watching the farmland give way to strip malls and, eventually, strip clubs when we arrived at the trailer park. As we pulled into Sleepy Hollow, I kept staring at the welcome sign posted just outside the chain-link fence:
    Sleepy Hollow Mobile Home Park
the sign read. It featured a picture of a large pine tree with two smaller pines in the foreground like a mother standing behind her two small children. There were no wintry pines in the neighborhood, so the picture made little sense outside of a clip art decoration meant to conjure up images of a breezy, woodsy home with a crackling fire to warm your toes after a long day's work as a forest ranger.

But the hominess of the sign was instantly negated by a chain-link fence that ran the perimeter of the trailer park. I saw this identical fencing about six months later when visiting Antoinette Davis in the North Carolina Correctional Institute for Women, but even without the comparison, it was the kind of fence that was meant to look mean and off-putting. The chain-link was tall, over six feet, but, for an added precaution, the owner of the trailer park, Brenda Davenport, had the fence people run barbed wire around the top. This gave it an extra growl. If any neighborhood needed a van promising a Brighter Image, it was this one. As we drove past the sign and the fence, I couldn't decide if it was meant to keep people out or to keep them in. On the night Shaniya Davis was kidnapped, that menacing fence did neither.

The main road into the neighborhood had been paved at one time but was mostly just a crumbling remnant of the solid surface it had once been. The park was set up like a human hand with the palm holding the main office and a dusty turnaround with all the trailers lined up diagonally off the fingers. The whole place was the color of dried dirt—the trailers, the cars parked outside the trailers and even the laundry hanging from sagging clotheslines made from shoelaces tied to together end to end. All of it dripped in that dull, lifeless, beige-brown color. Fayetteville isn't the prettiest town, but many of the streets are lined with happy green trees and some of the houses have that old Southern charm with their front porches and lazy swings inviting one to sit with an iced lemonade, speaking in low, sweet tones. But this trailer park felt more like an industrial wasteland or perhaps the set of a dystopian science-fiction film. All sense of light and life was left outside that barbed-wire fence. On the inside, it was just that brown, dusty earth with tired, brown trailers. The only exception were the bright green trash cans that rested haphazardly in the street, their hinged lids hanging open like panting dogs on a hot day. My husband drove through the park slowly, partially due to the potentially catastrophic potholes in the pavement and partially due to the dust we kicked up. It swirled around our car, serving as a visual representation of the despair we felt just by being there. When I saw a couple of kids tossing a ball back and forth near the park's office, I felt instantly guilty that I had the power to drive away from those oppressive homes housing people with oppressive problems, leaving those children to oppressive futures. We would drive back to Asheville and pull into a paved driveway nestled between bright patches of green grass and the start of a garden just off the back porch. Those kids tossing the ball on that scratchy earth would love the softness of our lawn, of our lives.

Dirt

THE POSHNESS OF my middle-class lifestyle was only the superficial reason for my guilt. Pity is a weapon reserved for the powerful. The most dangerous weapons disguise themselves as gifts. I had been on the receiving end of such a gift when I raised my own three kids in a neighborhood not especially dissimilar from the one we drove through now. Once a year we packed up our ragged belongings, piled them onto the back of a borrowed truck and moved to the same crumbling house on a different street. We existed among a population of people who lived the same way. Migration from house to house is a habit unique to the poor huddled inside city centers. Perhaps it is a testimony to our gasping optimism that we can, indeed, find greener grass over the next chain-link fence.

One unremarkable house stands at attention in my memory because it sat directly across from a crack house. That's what the white people called it. The black people called it "Liquor House," but both references held the same meaning. The house, like ours, sat on a dirt plot with cement steps serving as a front porch. I likely would not have noticed it as anything special had it not been for the mouse infestation in my own house. I am an indoor, sedentary person and only ended up on those front steps because I was afraid of the mice inside. At bedtime, I tied our hair up in tight knots, covering it in scarves to thwart the mice in their attempt to build nests in it while we slept. The daytime presented its own challenges; I walked in constant fear of a mouse running up my leg. So, for a few weeks that hot summer in Atlanta, I sat with my kids on the front stoop during those long scorching days. And because the exhaustion of poverty had long since stamped out my curiosity, I watched the neighbor's house out of boredom.

It was a busy house, a broken and dirty reflection of my own. Its front door had been smashed in before we moved into the neighborhood, which left only the iron screen door that banged against the frame each time someone entered. The screen was only partially connected to the door, causing it to wave like a ragged flag each time it slammed shut. The door banged with intense frequency that served as percussion to the loud but lyrical music that shouted through the windows and surrounded the property. Low riding cars pulled in and out of the driveway, expelling assortments of people from their interiors while collecting others who emerged from the house.

Many times a driver would simply honk his horn and one of the girls who stayed at the house would come running out. The car would pull away for twenty minutes or so and return with the girl who would run back into the house as the car backed out, she adjusting her skirt and he adjusting his zipper. There were always several children scattered about the front yard in parallel play to my own three kids who were doing the same thing in our dirt yard. I counted three women living in the house, but I could never sort out which child belonged to which mother. The women ran the place more as a community, running without discrimination to the yard to pick up a crying baby or running out to a car to service a very different kind of baby.

One man lived in the house. His role was more difficult to define. He spent most of his time tinkering under the hood of a car that felt permanent enough with its location to allow weeds to grow through the engine. He wore the same dingy white t-shirt nearly every day with the words:

Yo Bitch

written across the front like a challenge.

One day, when the woman who always waved to me was sitting on her own steps, I wandered across the street to her house. I brought a bag of Snickers Miniatures and offered her one as my kids tangled up with hers in the indiscriminate and accepting way children do. She accepted the candy bar, telling me her name was Latoya. She took a bite of the candy bar and chewed very slowly. Her nails were impossibly long. This made me think they harbored germs. However, I forgave her the long nails as I watched her eat in such a delicate manner, slowly moving the candy bar to her mouth, biting down with her straight movie star teeth, moving her hand back down to her lap with those long pink nails trailing like sparklers. After exchanging our names, we ate our candy bars without speaking. The kids played in the yard together, and we sat watching them with furtive glances toward each other until it was nap time. I said goodbye and walked back to my rodent-infested home. The next day she waved me over and from there we formed a little habit of stoop-sitting, a habit we continued for the three weeks it took to exterminate the mice.

Latoya was convinced, to the point of paranoia, that she was being surveilled by the FBI. She pointed to cars that drove down the street, identifying them as FBI agents. She told me she had her phone service shut off because she was certain they were bugging her house. Latoya made a convincing argument one day when a telephone repairman spent several hours in his cherry picker working on her phone line. We sat on her front stoop watching him watch us. "I ain't got no service, now you tell me why he's up there fiddling."

She had a tattoo decorating her perfect thigh. A man's name was written in large script letters. "Who's Daniel?" I asked her one day.

She was wearing pink shorts identical to her nail polish. They were tight, fitting themselves up against her body like happy, bright skin. She gently brushed the tattoo with her hand, "Oh, he's my baby's daddy."

I looked over the children playing in the yard; there were eight counting mine. I did not know how many mothers were represented there, among the children who were scratching in the dirt like chickens, but I knew that birthing armloads of children was common among the poor.

Poverty is referred to as *epidemic*, which means a widespread disease. Up until I earned my graduate degree, I had experienced two distinct poverties. The poverty of my early twenties through my thirties was a poverty of resources. I lacked sufficient resources to care for myself or my children. This type of poverty created a dependence in me. I depended on the church to provide blankets when our electricity was shut off; I depended on my government to provide food when my Tupperware sales were too low to fill the cupboards. The other type of poverty I experienced occurred within my middle-class childhood. It was a poverty of propriety. My father's house was impoverished by a lack of decency that produced lecherous and licentious behavior. This poverty created an independence in me. I became emotionally autonomous. Of my two experiences, I argue that the former poverty is endemic conditioning while the latter festers as a true epidemic, a disease which contaminates all those carefully contained within its yellow, sickly clutches.

The children playing in Latoya's little yard remained unaware that they were part of an endemic culture. I looked for the child Latoya had birthed with such hope and expectation. She told me he was called "Fat Daddy" and at first I conflated the nickname with Daniel and this made good sense to me as I knew Daniel to be a man with an excessive appetite even if that appetite was for women. It was much later that I learned that "Fat Daddy" was the legal name of her love child. "Where is Daniel now?" I asked, assuming he had abandoned her.

"Oh, he lives here," she said, nodding toward the house in her languid way. She was in love with the car-fixing guy wearing the dirty t-shirt?

I couldn't reconcile their living arrangement knowing that she made money riding in cars with hungry men. This surprised me. "But you sounded so sad when you said his name, I assumed he wasn't around," I pressed.

"Well, we're not together anymore," she told me. "He's with one of my housemates now. She's carrying his baby."

* * *

Later, the FBI, or some other governmental authority raided the house. Daniel was led out in handcuffs while a whole fleet of white people with clipboards fussed over the children who were at turns playing or crying. Several dark cars pulled away with children strapped into car seats, leading them to destinations that may or may not be worse than the one they were pulled from. Latoya wasn't home during the raid. She had answered a honk from a man inside a shiny car.

We successfully eradicated the mice from our house, but perhaps there was a more pervasive enemy living within the walls. I tended to my children each day, much like Latoya had tended to hers. We both were in sales and neither of us made enough money to cover the needs of our offspring. She fell for a thug who sold drugs and very likely pimped "his women" out for profit. I fell for a gay Christian who believed it was God's will to live a life of poverty in service to the poor. Every time we paraded in front of a church, begging for their tithes, we pimped out the poor for profit even if we believed that profit would be paid in the afterlife.

Later, the clipboard people assessed Antoinette's home and strapped the children from inside it into black cars bound for foster homes that may be festering with problems as complicated as 1116A Sleepy Hollow. I cannot know what caused the clipboard people to judge Latoya's home as deviant and mine as acceptable. Both lifestyles felt criminal to me.

Five Frail Steps

ANTOINETTE'S NEIGHBORHOOD IN Sleepy Hollow was familiar to me. I saw my own children in those boys tossing the ball in front of the trailer park's office. I watched one of the younger kids who watched me watch him when Simeon stopped the car. "This is it," my husband said over the whining noise of our air conditioner, "1116A." I broke my gaze from the little boy and turned to see Antoinette's trailer.

There was nothing outstanding about it; it held to the standard of monotony required of such neighborhoods. It stood in a line of identical trailers, all of them that dirty, unwashed brown color. Now that we were so close to it, I noticed how high off the ground they sat. I couldn't tell what they rested on, a trailer with wheels perhaps, but the bottom portion of the trailer was covered in what appeared to be sheets of grey copy paper taped together or maybe industrial rolls of aluminum paper wrapped around and around the bottoms of the trailers. But they sat high enough off the ground that each one required a stepping-stool staircase five steps high. The staircase outside Antoinette's house looked shaky, dangerous even. I thought of Mario McNeill carrying little sleepy Shaniya down those stairs at five o'clock in the morning and wondered how differently it would have all turned out if just one of those five steps had refused to support their burden and collapsed under McNeill's weight. But the weight of despair and the fragility of poverty had already placed Shaniya into a dangerous situation. At her sentencing, Antoinette said, "I didn't think about her surroundings, and I wish I would have. All I wanted was for her to be with me." But "being with" Antoinette meant living with a drug-using sister, Brenda, in a house that had no working plumbing. Being with Antoinette meant living in a trailer where a pedophile can climb five steps and be welcomed into a home because the drugs he carried in his pockets superseded the danger he carried in his head.

Hidden

McNeill was known locally as a drug dealer and also for his friendly relationship with the Davis family. McNeill doesn't elaborate on these relationships, possibly because he cannot make the distinction between business and personal connections. I read about this sort of thing happening with wealthy people. They don't know if those hanging about them do so because they genuinely like them, or because they genuinely like their money. It's easy to imagine McNeill struggling with this same distinction. He and his friends played duplicitous roles of buyer and seller. One side supplied the demand while the other demanded the supply. Perhaps he never knew if the Davis family, with all its brothers and sisters weaving in and out of McNeill's life in complicated, shifting relationships, befriended him based solely on his control over the candy bag.

But both McNeill and Brenda admit to a romantic relationship that mutated into a casual sexual affair that seemed to be accepted by all those who knew them. This feels like a betrayal to me. When I ask Antoinette about both Brenda and McNeill's lack of commitment and seemingly overt promiscuity, she dismisses it with, "They were always playing around. Brenda would cheat on him [her boyfriend JeRoy Smith] when he was in jail for drug-related crimes, and when he got out, he cheated on her." Antoinette had only lived in Brenda's trailer a few months before Shaniya was returned to her by Lockhart. JeRoy shared a room with Brenda, squeezing Antoinette and her two children, Carlesio and Shaniya, into the only other bedroom in the tiny trailer. The three adults and four children (counting Brenda's two children) were all smashed up against each other in 1116A Sleepy Hollow Trail. Additionally, both Antoinette and her youngest sister, Brenda, were pregnant the night Shaniya was kidnapped. The Davis family tree was a complicated and sometimes claustrophobic one. The family presented a certain cavalier if not callous attitude toward these tangled intimate relationships. That very night McNeill left his live-in girlfriend, April Autrey, to visit Brenda, his former girlfriend, only *after* he stopped by Tanisia's for "drinks and cards." And once he made his way to 1116A, there was Brenda waiting for him, yes, but there was also Brenda's live-in boyfriend, JeRoy, waiting there as well.

What about Autrey back at the house taking care of her two little children and McNeill's pet dogs? As many times as I re-order the events adding variables of apathy, devotion or desperation, I cannot make McNeill's life with Autrey cogent. It is illogical that a woman would date to the level of domestication and then kiss her lover goodbye each night as he trolls through the underbelly of Fayetteville like the Grinch, stealing kisses and lives in exchange for a drop of poison.

I can see what's in it for McNeill. There is a certain swagger associated with the neighborhood supplier.

McNeill lurked about with his long dreadlocks and his sharp brain, calculating the cost of doing business with impunity. All the players in this complicated social exchange would lose something. Be it money, self-respect, modesty, health, they would lose something with every transaction. And the inverse is true of McNeill. With every exchange of goods, he gained exponentially a higher return than their loss. He gained monetarily, yes, but this gain is not what sustained him. He also gained power and increased his control. The taxonomy of the relationships surrounding him show the complexity of his social structure. His world invited numerous classifications of nouns: lover, friend, girlfriend, buyer, brother, supplier. Prey. But even as these types, these representations of relationships swirled in and around his life, *his* classification remained consistent with each interaction. McNeill was always predator.

Although Autrey wasn't physically in the trailer that night, her place in the group was equally intertwined. Brenda and Autrey knew each other through shared boyfriends. So when McNeill asked to borrow her car to head over to Sleepy Hollow, Autrey understood not only what activities he planned, but also who he planned to do them with. I don't question Autrey's complicity in such an arrangement only because I understand her position of condoning outrageous behavior out of fear of rejection.

After I left my childhood home, I once was told to hide in a closet of a youth pastor's house when a parishioner unexpectedly came by for a visit. The youth pastor almost pushed me out of his bed and into the closet in panic. Once I was stuffed out of sight, he answered the door of his tiny house. I could tell by her voice that she was young, probably close to my age.

They sat at the table just feet away from where I stood naked with only a pressed board door between us. They talked for a while; her quiet voice felt like a whisper in my ear. She was wearing Loves' Musky Jasmine Flower perfume, which I could smell even as my own sweat began dripping down my back. I was afraid to swallow and I had to pee fiercely. He had a golf club crammed into the closet that, at first, felt cold against my leg. But as the time passed and the heat rose, the metal began to feel like a hot poker welting my thigh. When I was released from the closet, I actually examined my leg, expecting to see a burn mark there. I was nice to him, polite even, as I got dressed and walked toward the door that the girl had just passed through. I wished that we could have switched places. I wanted to be the young girl smelling fresh and pretty sitting at a table with a respected man saying a Christian prayer. Her world held no possibility of a naked girl hiding in a closet. I never went back to his little place in the woods. Years later, I saw a movie where Scarlett Johansson's character is pushed naked into a closet, and, when she is released, she comes out spitting mad, angrily gathering clothes yelling at the man that he had lost the privilege of seeing her, of touching her ever again. My mild-mannered exit offered complicity to the youth pastor's outrageous act, not unlike Autrey offering McNeill her car as a vehicle for his criminal acts and sexual indiscretions. McNeill was in her car only a few hours before his sexual indiscretions became criminal acts themselves.

> *For there is nothing hidden that will not be disclosed, and nothing concealed that will not be known or brought out into the open.*
> – Luke 8:17, New International Version

The Blue Blanket

MCNEILL EXHIBITED A languid, nonplussed attitude during the kidnapping of Shaniya Davis. There did not appear to be a fluster of emotion or adrenaline surge during his exit from the home with Shaniya in his arms. He did not hurry. This was no smash and grab. After relaxing inside Antoinette and Brenda's trailer for approximately two hours, McNeill calmly gathered the sleepy child and carried her down those five shaky steps to his girlfriend's car. Whether it was McNeill or Aunt Brenda, someone took some care and put some thought to her exit from the trailer, from her home.

Brenda Davis testified in court that Antoinette was sleeping when McNeill was in the home. She also testified that she, herself, was snuggled in her own bed. Her text messages betray her statements by showing an ongoing communication to and from McNeill during the time of Shaniya's abduction. Brenda, JeRoy and Mario McNeill were all awake and "partying" for at least two hours before Shaniya was taken. If Antoinette was awake for the party, her bloodstream did not show it. Her toxicology report came back negative from the medical examiner's office the next day. This information undermines the prosecution's theory that

Antoinette "did knowingly and with intent sell Shaniya Davis to Mario McNeill to cover a $200.00 drug debt." Antoinette was clearly inside the trailer that night, and, if she was not participating in the drug party, her sobriety makes her criminal charges even more alarming and certainly more damaging. It is likely she *was* sound asleep in her small bedroom, exhausted by working two jobs while pregnant. As with most issues involving Antoinette's actions from early that morning until six days later when Shaniya's body was found, nothing appears as this or as that.

Antoinette had just come off her shift from Carolina Inn at Village Green, which added to the argument that she was sleeping that night. She worked full time as a kitchen aide and was expected to clock back into work the next morning. It is reasonable to accept that she came home from a long day at work at a job that required physical labor, made dinner for the three small children who lived in the trailer and collapsed in bed. Antoinette was also five-weeks' pregnant at the time Shaniya was kidnapped, making Brenda's testimony, "My sister was asleep in bed when Mono [McNeill] came into the house," gain more credibility.

But Brenda's activities that night, although never examined as criminal, certainly can be seen as suspect. Brenda, along with her live-in boyfriend, JeRoy, were wide awake and, according to an FBI agent's testimony, texting McNeill, inviting him to party at their house. At some point during the early morning, McNeill collected Shaniya, who was sleeping on the sofa in the living room. He scooped her up in the blue blanket she was lying in, taking her into the cold February morning. I often think of all those hours McNeill was in the trailer, laughing and partying with Brenda and JeRoy before the kidnapping. Shaniya slept on the sofa right in the middle of the room. The trailer was small enough that perhaps McNeill moved Shaniya over, to make a place to sit down. He had almost two hours to either fight or fuel his sexual urges once he entered the trailer park. Some have argued that there was no battle for him, that he drove to Sleepy Hollow with the intent of kidnapping and raping Shaniya.

    The authorities certainly argue this point. A belief that Antoinette was involved in the crime is what put Antoinette in jail. Without McNeill's intention, Antoinette has no place in the crime. She serves no purpose. I argue that McNeill did wage a battle against himself that night. He was in the trailer park almost two hours before he even crossed the threshold to Shaniya's house. And then, even after entering, he smoked and drank for hours longer. These are not the actions of a premeditated rapist or a man depraved and acting upon a perverted instinct. His lengthy time in the Mitsubishi after driving into the neighborhood, his almost forty phone calls and texts sitting outside Shaniya's house, his unhurried visit with Shaniya's aunt, these actions all point to a man who had no plan and lacked intent or attempted to avoid or delay his intention.

    By all accounts, Shaniya was sleeping on the sofa because both of the bedrooms were full. Antoinette states that she slept in one room with her son on a pallet beside her. Brenda Davis and her boyfriend slept in the remaining bedroom with both her children. Shaniya was put in the last reasonable place to bed down, the living room sofa. But by sleeping there, rather than in the safety and privacy of a bedroom, Shaniya was put on center stage in the trailer. She was only wearing a baggy t-shirt and pink and white underwear, her little body in full view of a sexual predator for the several hours he was in the house. She was vulnerable and exposed even before she became aware that such things were possible. I worry over Shaniya during these hours with McNeill free to violate her visually. I want to take the blue blanket he later hides her in and tuck her under it, allowing it to protect and cover her.

I was revolted when, as a child in Sunday school, I learned of Noah's drunken antics. Noah was a fairly important character in the Old Testament, having saved the human race along with other living species from the devastating flood. Years after the water receded, Noah went back to farming, and of particular interest to him, he grew a vineyard. Through the seasons, Noah developed a penchant for a nip of his wine, becoming a functioning drunk. But once in a while, as is the way with addicts, he went too far. It was alarming enough that he drank wine to the point of passing out, but that he did it naked niggled at me. Right there in the old church classroom, sitting in metal folding chairs, all of the Bible School children were exposed to Noah's exposure.

Noah was sprawled in the family tent with young children running about and wives and mistresses busy with chores, stepping over and around him. There lay Noah, completely and thoroughly exposed. His youngest son, Ham, who saw him lying there on the floor of the tent, ran out and, possibly because he was a teenager or, more likely because he was mortified, grabbed his two older brothers. He tried to make sense of the situation by making fun of his dad. Shem and Japheth glanced into the tent to confirm their brother's story, but, being older, realized that there may be repercussions by adding a molehill to their father's proverbial mountain. So they backed into the tent, holding a robe and, with their eyes squished shut out of respect—or was it horror—dropped the robe to cover their father's nakedness.

When Noah woke up the next morning, hungover and cranky, the boys told him about Ham's gossip. Noah was so profoundly enraged that he put a curse on Ham and all his offspring for laughing at him and then, in a further attempt to punish Ham, offered a blessing to his older two boys for "covering his sins." I heard this saying many times during my indoctrination into the church. We were taught that it was our job as parishioners to "cover the sins of our fathers" in order to bring them glory. Noah responded like a typical addict. He behaved at best, poorly, and at worst, criminally, and when his youngest son, the only one with sense in the family, pointed out his outrageous behavior, it was Ham who was ridiculed and ostracized. The offender gathered his flock and judged the offended. I found this to be the case in my own father's house. Like Ham, I alerted my siblings to make them aware of our father's outrageous behavior, but like Noah, Glen craftily shifted the focus, galvanizing them to ostracize and judge me. *Something must be wrong with Abigail to say such things.* And there most assuredly *was* something wrong with Abigail. She spent her childhood like Shaniya spent her last night alive, exposed and violated, in desperate need of a protective covering. Through all my years of healing and forgiving, I remain unable to find a blanket large enough to cover the sins of my father.

But while I identify with Ham in the Bible, outcast and cursed for whistleblowing, in other words, the righteous one in the story, I also stand guilty as Noah, and therefore, McNeill. I have many times satisfied my thirst at the expense of another. McNeill raped and murdered a 5-year-old. These acts offend the sensibilities, and I can easily hide behind their hideousness to lessen the impact of my own insidious sins. My sins were less offensive and immeasurably less noticeable, yes, but how does one measure guilt? Does it come in degrees like murder or is it more of an all-or-nothing status?

Maybe Ham wasn't so righteous. I have gossiped about a friend to mutual friends, never more so than when inculcated in the church, attempting to garner their support in my judgment. We replaced "gossip" with "pray for," as in "Please pray for Jane; she is struggling with sexual fidelity to her husband," but the intent was the same. I once had a young Christian intern, who was living with us in London, walk into our little shared kitchen to ask for my forgiveness because he had "called me a bitch" to others in the group. He didn't really want my forgiveness; in fact, he did not believe he had sinned. Had he openly called me a bitch that day, I would have respected him and likely agreed with him. But he wilted behind the language by not only covertly calling me a bitch, but asking me to endorse his derision. And I was no different with a baby under one arm and collection plate under the other. My sin was swaddled in the sanctimony of the church, but its location did not negate its depravity.

Exposure and judgment: the deeper the crime of the other, the wider the distance from the convert to the condemned. I have long measured the space between crimes like McNeill's or Glen's and my own dark secrets as evidence of my own virtue. The longer the walk between my petty crimes and their revolting ones, the shinier the jewels in my crown. But if I am truly to fall naked before myself, I must acknowledge that my wretched condition is no more and no less tarnished than those who have fallen in the tent before me. I have managed to show restraint between thought and action but my nakedness is no less shameful than McNeill's.

Even with all that is known about this crime, much remains hidden. It remains unclear if McNeill intended to kill Shaniya when he gathered her into his arms early that morning. He refuses comment on the abduction other than to say, "The child's aunt asked that I take her to find her a good home where she could go to school." But given his proclivity for slaking his sexual satisfaction with children, it seems reasonable that he sat in that squalid living room, drinking unto drunkenness, with a constant bloodshot eye on Shaniya's body.

He entered the trailer park under the cover of the dark night, but he would commit the crimes of rape and murder in the light of day. As McNeill sat, first in his car, and then in the trailer, how those minutes must have ticked by in his head, each one representing restraint until sunrise, when he finally gave in to his impulses and took the child. Did he wait for daylight to expose his intentions, hoping to be noticed and therefore stopped? McNeill used Shaniya's blanket to cover her from the cold weather outside, showing a tenderness toward her. But as he drove slowly away from her house, her mother, her life, he began to feed his dragon. Less than two hours later, he would use that same blanket to cover his own sins. But the blanket, of course, was not large enough.

Muffin

It was a slow crime. The Sleepy Hollow surveillance cameras showed McNeill leaving the trailer park at 5:27 a.m. Despite the fact that he was now committing a federal offense of kidnapping, he surprisingly took his time driving to the exit, moving slowly through the chain-link fence out onto Murchison Road. He easily disappeared into disinterested early morning traffic. The drive from Shaniya's house to the Comfort Inn in Sanford, North Carolina, takes just under forty minutes. Shaniya was sick with a small fever that night, and so perhaps she mercifully slept during this sojourn. She was medicated with an over-the-counter medicine. Aunt Brenda either offered or McNeill took a bottle of Children's Motrin with him from the trailer because it rode in the car with Shaniya and McNeill.

This action, like the blanket, clouds interpretation. McNeill continues to make it difficult to cast him as an unequivocal villain. The Motrin, which was logged into evidence that was later presented at trial, offers a paradox. He took Shaniya, knowing she would suffer at his hands and yet grasped at a small offering to soften the suffering. The crime is easier to understand in the context of McNeill as a psychopath, but taking medicine from her home shows he is capable of sympathy. If he was unable to extract empathy from the bowels of his humanity, the rape and murder make more sense. There must have been a part of him that cared about her well-being, and yet how can this be as he continued to lazily and unhurriedly drive toward that hotel room where he would rape this little girl?

I am distressed by all of this languished horror. These last events in Shaniya's life are sluggish; they swim through the mud of confusion and despair. I understand this type of protracted pain. My father Glen was a slow tormentor, giving soft commands that required steady compliance. "Turn," or "Bend." Whispered verbs all quietly commanded. Time stretched out just when I needed it to truncate. Back in Sunday school, Jesus promised eternal life, but I wanted nothing of it. From my reluctant twist of the brass-plated door knob to Glen's room upon entrance to the reverse twist of the knob hours—was it years—later to exit, each moment suspended itself in eternity. Inside his room there was no beginning or middle or end. Time wouldn't follow the rules in his space. It bent and teased and froze and extended. When I think of Shaniya in that car, worried, fevered with illness and hot with fear, those moments must have stretched for her, each moment away from her home increasing to match the terror in her pounding heart.

When McNeill arrived at the hotel, he left Shaniya in the car while he went in to pay for his room. He made small talk with the clerk, telling her that he was traveling with his daughter. He said he was taking her to her mother's house in Virginia. The hotel clerk, Jacqueline Lee, was tired. This was the end of her eight-hour shift, and she was waiting for her coworker, Regina

Bacani, to clock in to take her place. She accepted his $98.00 and pushed a card key across the counter after writing "201" on the little paper envelope. It was 6:11 a.m. She dismissed the transaction from her mind until the following day. McNeill will likely never dismiss her. This observant clerk was the one who identified Shaniya from news reports and intelligently brought her suspicions to the police. Despite the fact that her first call to the hotline resulted in a busy signal, she persevered and, eventually, made a report. Had she not acted on her impulse, the surveillance footage may have been recorded over and McNeill could not be connected to this crime.

The police would need that video in that there would be no forensic evidence linking him to her death. Her body was too decomposed by the time it was found. The nail in McNeill's literal coffin is metaphorically provided for by the clerk who recognized McNeill and found his images on the security camera. The frame of McNeill holding the child in his arms while waiting for the elevator to take them to the second floor became the iconic theme for this case. It is the last known image taken of Shaniya, and it is a damning one for McNeill. He holds the barefooted, pantless child as a groom would carry his bride. Her arm crosses her body and her little hand rests on his shoulder, more in an effort to hang on than out of affection. She looks scared and vulnerable. Her feet are crossed at the ankles, not in a dangling relaxed way but in tension with her feet pointing up. She is rigid and protective, perhaps instinctive. The image haunts; the hunter holding his prey.

The elevator arrived. McNeill carried Shaniya into room 201. Once the door closed, a time clock began, counting down the minutes to her lost innocence and then, to her lost life. Shaniya had only two hours to live, and they would be gruesome ones.

McNeill was in the room only thirty-eight minutes. During interrogation he claimed that Shaniya watched *Sesame Street* while he got high. Thirty-eight minutes later, he was seen at the breakfast bar down in the lobby. He collected a juice, a muffin and a banana. This trip to the breakfast bar is devastating to me. He left this ravaged 5-year-old bleeding, bruised and broken in the hotel room alone. *Ravaged* is McNeill's term. Once he was incarcerated, waiting for his trial, he handwrote a note on prison stationary to the judge, saying, "I did not ravage Shaniya Davis." It's an unusual word, *ravage*, an extreme form of rape that goes beyond a violent physical act. *Rape* is an action verb, *ravage* is a crime of deeper dimensions. But it's an apt choice for McNeill. His rape damaged her unto devastation. Shaniya sat up in room 201, all alone and completely shattered while McNeill cruised through the breakfast bar line. He was never asked if the food was for Shaniya or himself, but in my version, the food *was* for her. An offering of a small crumb as an act of restitution.

When my sister and I were young, we played with the two Montgomery boys who lived across the street. Tim and Jim were close to our age, so we all easily fell in with one another. There was a large field behind their house that was lined with giant trees. We spent many hours up among their high branches, climbing and chasing and laughing in that abandoned, unfettered way of children. Once in a while, we slowed down, and each of us found a comfortable branch to stretch out on. We rested against the big fat trunk and traded jokes, shouting up to the kid who was highest in the tree who shouted back down like a vertical game of telephone. Once, Tim, the older boy, monkeyed his way up to the top branch while we all settled into our favorite spots below. My sister was above me on one of the branches when I heard her scream. I scrambled up the tree to see what had happened while Tim and Jim climbed down from their respective spots in the tree.

I got to her first. She was whimpering on the branch, holding her hand away from her like it was poisoned. I thought she had been bitten by a snake, although we had never heard of anything like that happening in an Ohio tree before. The boys got to her a few seconds after I did and Tim started in immediately with, "I'm so sorry!" He kept saying this over and over, and she just sat on that branch like she was in a coma. I couldn't make sense of the scene until Tim added, "I'm so sorry. I thought if I arched my back enough my pee would shoot out away from the tree!" My sister moaned, still holding her affected hand away from her body.

Jim couldn't understand why she had such a giant reaction, "So, you got a little pee on your hand, big deal," he said. But, somehow, Tim knew that his pee, splashed onto my sister's hand, felt like acid to her, and he wanted to fix it.

"I'm going to get you a Graham Cracker," he said as he nimbly transported himself down to the ground. The three of us watched him run across the field, and his frame become tiny as he entered his back door. We sat in silence, watching the back of his house until he emerged moments later waving a sleeve of Graham Crackers in the air like a white flag.

My sister was marked by Glen's emissions long before Tim's pee came innocently cascading down from the higher branch and splashed against her hand. I think she reacted so viscerally to him because out here, among safe childhood boys and the big trees and the scratchy bugs, out here, she was unprepared to be marked and sullied the way she was in Glen's house. By now, Jim had taken off his shirt and used it to dry her hand and this revived her somewhat. By the time Tim climbed back up the tree to meet us, my sister happily accepted the graham cracker as we all sat lined up on the big branch, swinging our feet. We were ready to believe that big problems could be solved by simple things.

Perhaps it was this idea that motivated McNeill to pick out a muffin for Shaniya. She sat up in that hotel room, marked and sullied as he ran down to the breakfast bar, attempting to assuage his selfish, sexual feasting with a crumb of contrition. But these are speculations. It's possible that after satisfying his sexual hunger, a physical hunger overtook him, and he ate the muffin on his way back to the room. No matter whose stomach it ended up in, both the guests of room 201 were now marked for death. The muffin became a symbolic last meal.

Asphyxiation

THE HUMAN BRAIN can survive up to four minutes when deprived of oxygen. Four minutes is a very long time. Men have run whole miles in four minutes. This is one of the reasons criminal profilers suggest that murder by asphyxiation is a personal one. It requires the murderer to maintain intimate physical contact with the victim for so many long ticks on the clock. Two hundred and forty of them. And it isn't just the length of time that offends; it is also a crime of uncomfortable proximity. Shaniya was savagely held close enough to McNeill that she could taste the sweat and dirt on his hands as they pressed into her mouth, blocking her air. She could look into his dark eyes with her own terrified ones as she struggled against him, a baby lamb in the claws of a wolf.

It is not difficult to argue that those last four minutes were the worst for her. She found herself once again assaulted at McNeill's hands, but this attack was different because Shaniya was different. When he first pushed her onto that bed in room 201, Shaniya was still an innocent. She might have been afraid of the things she knew, being away from her mom or the break in her daily pattern, but she could not be afraid of things she did not know. In the car on the way to the motel, and then again, at the elevator while held in McNeill's arms, Shaniya was terrified, most certainly, but it was a vague terror, one that had no true shape or form. After the rape, her terror could now be weighed and measured. She knew how it looked and how it felt. She would be able to identify its smell and these concrete memories formed and shaped a true terror which would be more devastating than her fearful instincts before the rape.

When Glen first invaded, it was a passive intrusion. My twin and I had just discovered sexual feelings but were too young to understand or identify them. Glen walked in on my sister rubbing herself in that childlike pre-sexual pleasurable way and demanded she continue while he watched. When he finished with her, he sent her to get me. "Daddy wants to watch you go up and down," she told me in a whisper. I remember her as a little ghost standing there in the pale pink nightgown with bright pink zigzag trim that grandma had sewn for all the cousins. Her face was white but not like milk or snow; those colors have a robust fullness that her face lacked. She was pale and watery; her hands were limp at her sides and her voice held a tremor that spoke like a prophecy. *Up and down* was the term we used for our awkward self-explorations. I was immediately hot and felt a burning between my legs that heated me all the way to my face. I knew better than to question such things and so went to his bedroom where he sat on his bed waiting for me. He told to me to "go up and down" while he watched. Our words, once so innocent and free, fell rotten from his mouth. He gestured for me to lay on his bed beside him. I was scared but trapped. I lay beside him and began moving around, trying to just reveal enough to please him and make it all stop but knowing at that moment on his green bedspread that it never would. He asked me all kind of questions while I squirmed around next to him: Why did I lie on my stomach? What did I think about? I was consumed by confusion and that burning pain between my legs felt intense and unbearable. Our family had frequent bonfires and after that night I could never watch him skewer his hotdog and hold it over the flame, slowly turning it until the juices bubbled up and spilled into the fire without feeling that heat sear between my legs and run up through my stomach and into my mouth. I couldn't identify it at the time, but later, I recognized it as shame. It would become my constant companion in his house.

But that first night, lying on his bed with my nightdress pulled up, exposing my underwear, I was flustered and embarrassed. He just sat there without moving, asking his quiet questions. I finally told him that when I went up and down I thought about dancing. This did not inspire him and so he asked again. I told him I imagined walking out to the mailbox and back which was also a lie, but it seemed to satisfy him. When it was over he told me it was a bad thing that I had done and that it was only okay if I did it in front of him. I was to never go up and down without him again.

And so began those many years of being called into his room. Before that day, before he took away our pureness, he would call us to his room with his quiet, "Girls," and we would go to him, not knowing how dark and unsanctified his chamber would become. But after that day, his whispered "girls" would grip us in fear and cloak us in shame. The knowledge that such things were possible was almost more paralyzing than the things themselves.

The assault on Shaniya's body, as damaging and destructive as it was, was no match for the assault on her mind. After the rape, Shaniya was forced into an awakening that revealed a world she could not have imagined before she was lifted from that sofa. It was a knowledge that her small shoulders were not strong enough to bear. So, by the time McNeill came after her a second time, this time to use his hands for murder, Shaniya recognized that a new pain, a previously unfathomable level of darkness was possible. And as she watched him approach her for the second time, she saw this pain as probable and inescapable. It would be impossible for her brain to settle back into the childish thoughts and imaginings that filled her innocent head before his rape. The rape defiled her body but the knowledge of the rape defiled her mind.

The eight or so minutes that McNeill left her sitting in that hotel room all alone while he went down to the lobby for breakfast are challenging to consider. Did she collapse from exhaustion and pure devastation? McNeill left her alone at the time she normally would just be waking up for her day. As much as I want to see her sleeping there, a little angel on that profaned bed, it seems unlikely. McNeill sprang from his hiding place and launched his attack, leaving Shaniya wounded but alive as he slunk away to the watering hole. Although it was a repellent enlightenment, Shaniya was now educated that such things can occur. And once awakened to such horrors, sleep would become her enemy. She would need to remain alert and aware to protect herself from future attacks. And even if she were lucky and able to get to sleep, he could easily hunt and haunt her there.

Rape is not a singular act. It blends into a cacophony of memories and realities, becoming the musical score to the montage of life. Had Shaniya lived a long life, the life the world hoped for her, she would have found her way to healing and forgiveness. She could have moved from survivor to thriver. But the rape would always be a demarcation. Each thrust of his lust separated her from her innocence irrevocably. And there Shaniya remained, in a perpetual interstitial space, the time after the rape and before the murder. She was suspended in the shattering. Thus, when he approached her that second time to kill her, she now had knowledge. When God told Adam and Eve in the garden that they would die if they ate from the tree of the knowledge of good and evil, I can see his motive as a compassionate one. It wasn't the actual acts of evil that would kill, what would undo them was the knowledge that evil existed.

* * *

That he asphyxiated her is not in dispute, but there are differing reports about when and where McNeill murdered Shaniya. The police ultimately settled on a theory that left Shaniya alive after leaving the hotel room. Seth Chambers provided an eye-witness testimony in court when he told the jury that he saw Shaniya alive at 7:11 a.m. He was also a guest at the Comfort Inn that night. In the morning, he was on his way out to his job for American South General Contractors but ran back to his room on the second floor because he had forgotten his receipt. His timeline is validated by McNeill's check out time but his actual account is questionable. He testified that he "saw Shaniya in that man's arms [here he was asked to identify the defendant in the courtroom] and she was alive." He goes on to say that he noticed them only because McNeill was carrying her in such an odd manner. She was partially obstructed by a blue blanket but he paid attention because of the way McNeill held her draped across his arms but high up on his chest in a way that is not comfortable for either the holder or the one being held. He said he saw Shaniya's arm raise up, slowly and then fall back down. He passed them in the hall and didn't consider them again until two days later when Shaniya's face lit up national television.

It could have been possible for Chambers to see Shaniya's body moving as a natural physical reaction of being attached to a moving object, like a dead fish moving with the current of a lake. I believe that Shaniya did not leave that hotel room alive. But even if she did, she had minutes, not hours, to live. McNeill is seen by the Comfort Inn maintenance man, lying the child covered in the blanket in the back seat of the black Mitsubishi. The maintenance man assumed the girl was sleeping because, to his credit, no other possibility was available to his brain. But if Shaniya was not murdered in the hotel room, then she was murdered in April Autrey's car less than twenty minutes later.

McNeill started the trip back to Fayetteville, stopping just shy of the halfway mark, and walked back off Highway 87 about one hundred feet where he dropped her body onto the earth. He rolled a broken tree branch on top of her. It would take four hours for the search and rescue team to remove it from her body. McNeill returned to the car and drove home. As he arrived, his two young children were filling their lungs with the oxygen that he deprived Shaniya of less than an hour before. They yawned and stretched awake from their warm safe beds just as a cold morning rain began to fall on Shaniya's body.

He was oppressed and afflicted, yet he did not open his mouth; he was led like a lamb to the slaughter, and as a sheep before its shearers is silent, so he did not open his mouth.
  – Isaiah 53:7, New International Version

Lamb to the Slaughter

IN THE BURNING heat of the years that were dedicated to Blood-n-Fire, we moved into the condemned warehouse that served as headquarters for upper echelon leadership, the sanctuary for the church and the homeless shelter itself. The place was enormous, five stories shooting up from a section of the sprawling first floor, which covered the space of a city block. Broken up weedy cement surrounded the whole structure outside, and this industrial decay was mirrored on the inside, which was a dangerous labyrinth of crumbling walls, oil-stained floors, busted out windows and fire-escapes that held onto the building by one or two rusty bolts. There was a makeshift kitchen, possibly used to serve the warehouse workers a hot lunch back in its day. It was reminiscent of old clips of European buildings that had been bombed during World War II. There were layers of dust on all the surfaces. The two massive pots—my three kids could and did hide inside, so great their size—which were called into service for every meal, took two men to haul up on the kerosene-fueled hot rings used for all the cooking. The rats were a constant nuisance. None of the food was stored in the kitchen but in a back section of the warehouse that had been walled off and secured by multiple locks and chains across its main door. But this did not stop the rats from sniffing about, leaving biological evidence of their presence in little trails of black pebbles. Sometimes, hairs from their fur would be stuck to a greasy surface or the side of a pan. A rumor floated around that, before our time, the previous kitchen manager locked a cat in the kitchen overnight to secure the territory free from rats. But when he returned in the morning, the cat was dead, left as a bony carcass eaten by a swarm of frenzied rats. But the kitchen was just the rats' playroom; the rats lived and bred inside the monstrous pantry at the far end of the warehouse. Behind these locked doors, despite the smell of rotting food and rat urine, lay the treasures of the ministry.

It was the only room in the warehouse with a twenty-four-hour-a-day guard. These guards were found among those who slept in the warehouse shelter. The job rotated every so often because the men, by nature of their homeless status, were transient. But the job was a coveted one because it came with authority and a big ring of jangling keys worn like a sheriff's badge around the warehouse. Impotence is an inherent condition of homelessness and any type of authority, no matter how trite, was sought after and fought for. The job came with a private cot tucked away inside the massive pantry and free reign over the inventory. In a society where cash is in short supply, currency becomes creative. The warehouse pantry operated like a bank vault with large container trucks unloading their overstocked or expired goods off the loading dock in the back. Those long semi-trucks would pull in from every kind of store. From McDonalds, we had pallets full of the kid's meal toys, thousands of cartoon characters wrapped in plastic piled into high towers, their eyes eerily fixed to different locations in the pantry like in a Stephen King movie. Nabisco and even the elves of Keebler unloaded their unsold merchandise into our mighty pantry. All these goods were either rotting perishables, expired shelf goods or generally useless. The pantry became the island of misfit toys with the pantry guard playing the role of a street-smart Santa who could exchange the mountains of merchandise into a profitable business.

But all that nonsense changed when Phil took over. He was one of those grizzled homeless men with a long, yellowed beard and eyes set so far back into his head that I wondered how he could see past his facial bones. Phil was handed the keys one random day; perhaps the previous guard was in jail or off on a binge with a pipe full of crack he bought with forty boxes of Hostess Ho Hos. Phil took the job seriously and ran it with an integrity the ministry itself would have been wise to adopt. No more of these blackmarket, backroom deals under Phil's careful watch. He kept the job and his loyalty to the position and his leader, David VanCronkite, until VanCronkite sold the whole business to Georgia State University. VanCronkite invested his proceeds into "ministry properties" around Georgia and North Carolina, but in my version, a big, fat check went out to old Phil who stood as loyal sentry for so many unpaid years.

But long before there was any thought of Georgia State University football fields, Jeff Batton and I moved into the second floor of the warehouse to oversee the outreach ministry. We gave away all of our belongings (except my books) and moved with our three small children into a "loft" one floor up from the shelter. There was no running water, no plumbing and no kitchen. We "made do" with a microwave and a refrigerator, but because we had no proper income and relied on God to pay us, both of our appliances sat empty during our time there. God didn't seem especially interested in fresh produce or diapers for his toiling workers.

My children were all young, the oldest just starting kindergarten and the youngest a crawling baby. The conditions were harsh and the children were in constant danger. Even when the warehouse was in its prime, operating as an industrial work site, it was never zoned for or intended to house humans. Our loft was one large corner of the warehouse sectioned off from the main floor with a long wall of drywall. The children were filthy, their clothes and hands always covered with the industrial grime of the warehouse. My youngest, Jake, looked like an Okie during the Dust Bowl. He moved around the coated floors like a sponge, soaking up the dirt into his clothes and hair and lungs.

We slept in the large open space of our loft and from my bed I could see the children's bunk beds across the room. The two youngest slept together in the bottom bunk and my first born, Alex, a kindergartner, earned the top. Many mornings I would wake up and see Alex's arm pointing up to the ceiling from her bed, following the route of one of the rats who ran along the pipes in the ceiling. I can still see her tiny arm raised from her body as she lay in a bed that very likely was stained with rat pee. She was so calm, following a rat with her pointer like a morning devotion.

Among the discarded projects littering the warehouse there lay a hidden gem, or so it looked to me. Between the long walk from the kitchen to the pantry there was an unassuming door to the right which opened into a large landfill for clothing. Once upon a time, several years before we arrived, someone attempted to organize a clothing donation room. The room was quite large, about 1500 square feet, and it was covered in piles of clothes. At one time there were racks, which were now pulled down onto their sides with clothes under and above them. The room was full of mold and grime and I wanted it. I envisioned a clean, tidy clothes closet that the women of the shelter could wander through and exchange their own ratty, dirty clothes for the pretty, clean ones in my new gigantic closet. I felt that a saucy skirt and a fresh cotton shirt could increase their self-worth and offer a tiny flame of optimism in their otherwise dark, cavernous lives.

I fully intended to use the closet myself, and so it was also my own darkness that led me to find this brighter solution. It was going to be a massive job and one I nearly didn't finish. Each morning, after breakfast of corn dogs or whatever the latest donation truck had dropped off (but mostly corn dogs), I grabbed Jake and carried him down the flight of stairs to the clothing closet. He was new to crawling, and I felt comfortable letting him explore the wide area while I began the physical task of pulling all of the clothes out of the big room. I followed a general system of piling clothes into separate categories, one for skirts, one for shoes, one for sweaters, and so began the long process of handling each item—most of which were as ratty and dirty as the clothes I had hoped to replace—and tossing them into their designated areas. The piles sprouted and grew like the kudzu vines that had overtaken parts of the upper floors.

It took me three weeks to empty out the room entirely. The warehouse space in front of my closet now held large piles of clothing, some of which were over six feet tall. They made a great playground for Jake, who would crawl between the piles, squealing as I sporadically chased him around the clothing mountains. Mostly, I let him play on his own while I tended to my work. When the room was finally emptied, I set to sweeping out the floors which were thick with dust-coated oily patches and miscellaneous items among which could have been used hypodermic needles. I didn't consider any of the dangers at the time; this would come after the incident.

I was so excited to finally have the space emptied out and had my mind set on bleach and then paint before I put the whole thing back together again. But this was a large space and sweeping it out with a defective old broom was ineffective and frustrating. I became focused on finishing the task when I realized I hadn't seen Jake in a while. I stopped sweeping. The room was swirling with fine dust particles, and the floor held several splotchy piles of dirt and trash. I must have been working for some time and was nearly done. Where was Jake?

I wasn't overly alarmed. He was only a crawling child and could not have traveled a great distance. I assumed I'd find him playing around the piles of clothes. "Jakey," I called playfully. There was only quiet. I tried his nickname. "Coby," I called out. "Where are you?" No answer. I ran around all the piles; Jake was not among them. My heart started beating in that frantic, primal way. I had a thought that he had somehow burrowed under one of the piles and that he was hidden underneath. It was so hot inside the warehouse, sometimes swelling up to one hundred degrees, that I imagined him fainting from heat stroke under a pile of men's sweaty jackets. I began clawing at the piles, looking for little holes he could have crawled into. "JAKE!" I cried out. Silence. With all that noise and all those people with busy industry in and out of the warehouse each day, the whole floor from the pantry to the kitchen was uncharacteristically silent. Nothing moved but the dust swirling in the air that had escaped my room and now filtered through the floor. I stopped throwing clothes around, thinking it was unlikely that he was pressed into unconsciousness under one of the heavy piles of filth and rot. I looked to my right, toward the pantry.

The only place available for him to crawl out of my view was an industrial freight elevator. It was a giant elevator, large enough to house my entire family comfortably. But the elevators didn't work and besides, the door to get in required pushing a set of large buttons that were too high for his little hands to reach. And even if he had climbed up on something and pushed the bright green button, physics and logic would be against him in that the protective door covering the caged elevator door was too heavy for even me to open alone. He had not crawled back toward the pantry, and this was the bad news. Had he gone in that direction, he would have been contained, but the direction toward the kitchen, on my left, opened out into a community dining room and from there, a huge door out to the parking lot. Now I was panicked.

About the time I started on my clothing room closet project, a woman had been charged with selling her newborn baby girl in exchange for some drugs. She had made the exchange on the notorious corner of Ashby and Simpson. This corner was a few blocks away from the warehouse and was such a well-known drug center that Blood-n-Fire had started a satellite outreach there on Saturday nights. They had loaded up all the speakers and subwoofers along with the giant barbeque grills and threw a big Christian Party every Saturday. The music pounded out of the speakers while the ladies and gentlemen of the neighborhood lined up with Styrofoam plates (never out of supply in the pantry) for their barbeque chicken sandwich and bag of potato chips (usually generic but sometimes Lays). Phil occasionally sent big gallons of McDonaldland toys for the little children unfortunate enough to spend the evening on a street corner that oversaw an average of one murder a week. Both the stolen baby, who was found sleeping and safe, and the man who bought her were placed into State custody, but the mother was never found. Perhaps she, too, was in State care with a Jane Doe tag tied to her big toe and cause of death listed as "overdose."

But this event, a peripheral consideration up until now, came running to my frontal cortex with such force that I dropped to the ground among the discarded clothes. Someone had stolen Jake and they were going to sell him on Ashby and Simpson. Such was my conviction that I ran the whole length of the warehouse screaming, "Jake has been stolen! My baby is gone!" until I reached the parking lot. The lot was a hangout place where the homeless men and women spent their time waiting for either the shelter to open at six p.m. or for the lunch line to open at twelve. There was always a cluster of people sitting up on a wall that lined the parking lot. Homeless people tend to carry big bags of their belongings, many times using black garbage bags to transport their possessions from cat hole to cat hole. I ran out of the warehouse and saw them all looking at me. I had been screaming just seconds before but when I got to the lot I calmed down immediately. Jake was in one of their bags, I was certain of it, and I needed a strategy to get him back safely. By now some of the second floor team had come down, alerted by my screams. I pointed to the row of ne'er-do-wells. "Check their bags," I said calmly. "One of them has Jake inside. They are going to try to sell him on Ashby and Simpson." No one on the team questioned me; they simply walked up to the group against the wall and asked for them to open their bags. All the homeless people complied; again, none of them questioned or protested. They must have been so accustomed to harassment that even minor forms of it became something they acquiesced to and accepted.

While they were spilling their clothes and personals onto the public parking lot, a police car pulled up. Someone had called 911 when I was screaming through the warehouse. This was going to require an intelligent delicacy because we were not legally permitted to live within the warehouse. How was I going to explain to the police officer that I had lost my child inside a condemned warehouse that served as a ministry hub to crack-addicted street-sleepers? I could be arrested, among other things, for endangerment of a child. If Jake were to be found on Ashby and Simpson or somewhere inside a black bag on his way to Ashby and Simpson I could be charged as an accomplice to human trafficking or sexual servitude of a minor. Never mind that my role in these events may have been unwitting, the law holds no distinctions. As Antoinette learned in the bowels of the Fayetteville Police Department while under interrogation, ignorance does not negate culpability.

I spoke with the police officer, careful to indicate that I was volunteering inside with my baby boy and not actually living there. Standing on the outside of the building, as I was now, I saw the landscape as the officer might. Homeless people huddled in groups on the front dock and scattered along the parking lot wall, the fire escape dangling from the third floor, bits of trash discarded on the dilapidated steps. Had the police officer showed even the slightest amount of judgment, as the one who showed up to Antoinette's trailer, I would have been hauled into the police station and charged with very serious felonies. I was a negligent parent who created a pattern of bad decisions that consistently placed my children in danger—real, true-life-threatening danger. My story looked better, I suppose, in that I was white, articulate and working as a missionary. Although when I hear that term used as a job descriptor now, *missionary*, I cringe at its implications. I can hear the false pride and understand the charade of that job. I used it as a get-out-of-jail-free card.

The police officer was pacified, VanCronkite had come down from the heavenlies by this point, and even the hard core Atlanta police force found his charm to be irresistible. Someone called down from the fifth floor balcony that he had found Jake up there in the elevator shaft. We all ran up the five flights and there was Jake, filthy but content in the arms of a stranger. I knew he could not have ridden the elevator up to this floor, which meant I also knew that he had been carried there. There was such a constant stream of people, both the homeless and the workers, that I couldn't know who carried him up here and held him captive for the hour and ten minutes that he was missing. Nor could I know the person's motives, meaning I could not know the degree of harm, if any. Jake was too young to speak and so the unasked questions remained unanswered. The police officer left without even filing a report, and the stranger on the fifth floor, was he the saint or the monster, handed my baby son back to me. I could see through the streaks in the dirt on his face that he had been crying at some point, but whatever had happened to him held enough distance for the tears to dry and for those salty paths to be covered with still more dirt.

Had this event altered me, had I chosen at that moment to pack up my children and exchange the warehouse for a tiny apartment where I would live in poverty but this time as a student, maybe, maybe, my crimes up to this point could be forgiven. But because I would not be altered, I would eventually be broken, and in my brokenness, so too would go my children. It would take me five more years to leave this *ministry*, this lifestyle of extremes and deprivation. I find these remaining five years unconscionable. When Antoinette stood in front the honorable Judge Ammons, she admitted only to one crime. "I wanted Shaniya with me and her big brother," she told him. "I didn't think about her circumstances, and I guess I should have." My life's trajectory did not land me in front of a judge Ammons, but I hold an open court in my own head where I mouth Antoinette's words over and over. *I should have considered their circumstances.* In my courtroom, the gavel falls on "guilty." Like Shaniya's blue blanket, there was no cover large enough to cloak my sanctified sins.

Behold, I will gather you to your fathers, and you shall be gathered to your grave in peace, and your eyes shall not see all the evil that I will bring upon this place and its inhabitants.
– 2 Chronicles 34–28, *New International Version*

Thousands of Bones

SHANIYA'S ORIGINAL RESTING place was most indecorous. Highway 87 runs between Fayetteville and Sanford, North Carolina. It is a desolate thruway, one that provides long stretches of road bordered by more shrub than tree. These rangey sections suddenly open to the gentleman's clubs and pawn shops that occasionally dot the state road, making them appear like scratchy intrusions on an otherwise quiet and lonely pocket of the world. It's surprising that so many strip clubs can survive within such close proximity to one another. Even their names crowd one another with *Snarky's Sports Bar* separated from *Sharky's Cabaret* with only the modest *Pearl Necklace* pushed between them. Their monotony is broken up by the check-cashing shops, which are snuggled up to pawn shops like a tandem bike. It was off this highway, at the crossroads between Lee and Harnett County, where Shaniya was first buried. "Buried" is a generous word to describe how she was left. She was found above the ground, wearing only an adult-sized black sweatshirt and her pink and white underwear. Her own white shirt, worn when she was torn from her house, was never recovered. It's notable that she left her house in a color conveying purity and innocence and was left at the dumpsite in a color denoting McNeill's transgression. The black shirt that she was found in was likely the same one McNeill was wearing in the surveillance video from the Comfort Inn. The sweatshirt adds another contradictory slant to the profile of a cruel murderer.

It was cold out that morning and McNeill would have had to physically take the black shirt off and place it on Shaniya, choosing to offer her comfort at his expense. If Shaniya was already dead by the time he arrived at this remote spot off Highway 87, it is possible he put the shirt on her as a burial shroud. If she was alive when she left the hotel, perhaps he put his shirt on her after the rape to keep her warm once they left the hotel. Both scenarios are disturbing because they inconvenience a tidy judgment against McNeill. The black shirt was not draped over her like a blanket but rather worn by her. He physically dressed her in this garment. He may have placed her inside his shirt as one final marking of her before he left her body out in the cold morning air. Perhaps the shirt was a symbol of possession.

Once he arrived at his chosen burial ground, he dragged a heavy tree branch over her body as a partial covering. Shaniya's feet were bare. It was her tiny feet that the searchers first saw peeking out through the thick foliage. They were led to her by a cadaver dog. Max was fresh out of the canine-training unit. He found Shaniya's body on his first day on the job. That he discovered her is a relieving epilogue to her murder. Shaniya's body was violated and exposed. She was cold and decomposing. He was an enthusiastic dog, and his frisky, playful demeanor seemed more suited to Shaniya than if she had been found by one of the heartbroken women or men on the search team. Max's job was macabre, yes, but his presence there in the scrubby underbrush also offers solace. It is fitting that this child, broken and forever lost, could be recovered by the one member of the Search and Rescue team who could hold no sorrow. There is a small amount of restitution in this act. Max first encountered her bare foot, which was resting in a small stream of water. This also is a comforting image. The water symbolically cleansed her with its rhythmic flow. It's significant, too, that it was her foot that was first seen by the team. The only distinguishing characteristic included on her Amber Alert from six days previously was a small scar on her left foot. And so, when the rescuers saw that little foot dangling, they needed no DNA lab results to confirm what they did not want to know. This child was Shaniya Davis.

Another consolation that her first grave site offers is that she was not alone. During the six days she lay there, there were thousands of bones there with her. The spot was used by hunters to field dress the deer they had shot. And so Shaniya rested with prey, who, like her, had been hunted and killed by their predators.

The Human Condition

SHANIYA WAS REPORTED missing on Tuesday, November 10, just before seven in the morning. She wasn't found until six days later at 4:45 in the afternoon, Monday, November 16. It took six days to find her, allowing the Fayetteville Police Department to establish a task force and rightfully call "dibs" on the investigation. Because her body was found "on the Lee/Harnett County line," there was a brief skirmish between police jurisdictions. But the Fayetteville Police Department took lead on the case with all officers from both counties reporting to the Task Force in Cumberland County. The Task Force was made of twenty people who included police detectives and local social service workers. Teresa Chance, the Public Information Officer, was the natural spokeswoman for the Task Force but quickly found herself out of her depth when reporting to national television outlets.

The Task Force suffered a blow to their ethos when, less than twenty-four hours after Antoinette's 911 call, they arrested Clarence Coe. The police already had Coe in their sights for an unsolved and unrelated murder (no formal charge ever came from those suspicions), but he was arrested because of Antoinette Davis' fear-based concession to the police. After their initial visit to Davis following her 911 call, the police held Antoinette in a faux custody arrangement, demanding she tell them who had the child. They were convinced she withheld information about Shaniya's whereabouts and conducted four separate interviews with her up to six hours each. Davis, cold, hungry, terrified and pregnant, finally conceded to them that Coe had struck Shaniya on her left cheek, which knocked her to the floor. She claimed he then bent down, scooped her up and left the trailer with Shaniya in his arms. Coe was Davis' then-boyfriend and also was the father of the child she was carrying. Coe was arrested briefly. But just a day later, McNeill was seen on the Comfort Inn surveillance video holding Shaniya in just the same way Davis had accused Coe. The police released Coe, but he was spitting mad and vowed to the national media that he would sue the county for false imprisonment. He will have to wait until March 2018 because he was arrested for the unrelated crime of felony breaking and entering and sentenced to seven years and five months in the Central Prison of Raleigh, North Carolina. He will be unable to sue the county government until he serves his time and loses his status as a ward of the State. Although Coe was not Shaniya's kidnapper or rapist, Shaniya's body held an eerie legacy to him. The medical examiner found a bruise on her left cheek exactly where Antoinette told police Coe had hit her. Perhaps Coe did strike the child earlier that night and then stormed away alone.

Someone certainly struck her, and the idea is a depressing one, adding to the chaos and harm that Shaniya endured during her four-week stay at 1116A Sleepy Hollow Drive. What a day of absolute woe and devastation for the child! In her last twenty-four hours alive, her mom, away at work, left her, according to Antoinette, in the care of her "drug-addled aunt." Shaniya stayed in a trailer that had no working plumbing; she was struck in the face so hard she collapsed to the ground and then six or so hours later was awakened from sleep, kidnapped, raped and then murdered.

Poverty, indifference and betrayal submerged this child in an ocean with a current too strong for her to overcome. Even as she thrashed about, attempting to strengthen the muscles required to survive in such a hostile, dangerous environment, the predators came prowling. Her life with her suburban father was not much different. With his risky lifestyle choices and wild frat boy parties with prostitutes purchased with ease and frequency, Shaniya had no lifeboat to buoy in these dark waters. Her rape and murder were devastating even if they were unsurprising. The National Center for the Review and Prevention of Child Deaths reports that 1,700 children die each year as the result of child abuse or neglect. Of these deaths, 87% are female. Shaniya's death would add to North Carolina's child homicide report, which reached 36 children by the end of 2009. And these numbers are arguably low considering that 206 children's deaths were attributed to accidents that year. Many of these children may have actually died as the result of neglect or intentional harm.

Add to this the alarming statistics that one in four girls will experience sexual abuse by time they turn 18. Suddenly Shaniya's rape and murder point to a disease that may not have festered and grown in that filthy trailer but rather is systemic in nature. The circulatory system of the human collective is creating a fungus so foul and sophisticated that it does not kill those who carry the disease, but rather those innocents who come in contact with the infected. The nationally collected data reveal that neither deep poverty nor lack of education causes child homicide and child rape. Americans prefer the myth that such things happen in the bowels of the trailer parks, but this myth is simply to assuage those outside of the conditions of poverty. We want to pass off such perversion as happening in a geographic and economic world away from our own. But this is not the case.

Shaniya is a shining example of this misconception. She straddled a life of privilege with her wealthy, white father and a life of indisputable poverty with her poor, black mother. But this child experienced depravity from both sides of her family lineage. And in the end, the collection of selfish decisions on both sides of her parentage contributed to her wrenching death. Shaniya's murder may not have been preventable, but it was most assuredly predictable. While McNeill performed the final physical act of murder, her parents, her teachers, the Department of Family Services and any human who has pushed down the impulse to inquire into a situation that felt off or wrong hold some sort of collective culpability in her murder. She did not die as the result of a shocking set of unique and specific circumstances. Her life's narrative was written and read by all of us long before it happened.

> *A mighty fortress is our God, a bulwark never failing; Our helper He, amid the flood of mortal ills prevailing.*
> – Martin Luther, 1529

A Mighty Fortress

WHILE ANTOINETTE AND her sisters carved out a life for themselves at their grandmother's house and under the misfocused eye of DSS, one of the neighborhood boys showed some promising talents. Juanita McNeill Ball raised her three kids in the scratchier part of Fayetteville, North Carolina. Mario was her second born and by all accounts, her quietest child. Ball was a single mother and found a warm welcome and authentic acceptance at the First Baptist Church of Fayetteville. She soon joined the church and began singing soprano in the church choir. Her children, however, did not join her on Sunday mornings, preferring instead to sleep in after a long week at school. It wasn't until Mario was a young teenager that he showed interest in the First Baptist Church. Roy Birch, one of the pastors there, started a neighborhood softball team that practiced on the church grounds. It was this team that attracted Mario. Birch is a soft-spoken man who takes a pause before responding to all my questions. We spoke by phone, and, like the other members of his church I had interviewed, he approached me with the caution of a trained sentry.

I unsuccessfully searched for the reverend at the First Baptist Church of Fayetteville on our first research trip. It was an imposing building, thousands of bricks interrupted by two tidy rows of tinted windows. The doors were locked but clicked open by an unseen hand after I gazed into a camera box. I was expecting to find Roy Birch inside. According to news reports, Birch was a reverend here who knew McNeill well enough, intimately enough, that the defense team called him to speak at sentencing. McNeill's mother, Juanita Ball, was also on hand to plead the court's mercy by not sentencing her son to death. But McNeill, for reasons he held in his heart, denied both his mother and his former pastor the opportunity to speak on his behalf. McNeill would allow no one to stand for him, telling the judge, "My goal was freedom, I lost my freedom. What does it matter after that?" He would not argue against the death penalty, and, unsurprisingly, the jury recommended just that. I wanted to speak with Birch, to hear what he would have said, had McNeill allowed him to speak in court that day. I was unprepared for what I found at the church.

It was a massive brick structure nestled into the community like an armory. The enormous building dissected itself with an architectural timeline. What must have been the original church was a modest brick, loaf-pan type structure that is typical in old chapels. The two long sides held six enormous stained-glass windows with a larger, majestic stained glass at the entrance. The windows were all bordered with thick wooden frames painted a cheerful white. But the loaf pan smashed into an unfortunate renovation in the 1980s when the design sensibilities leaned more toward utility and less toward ornate. It was into this long, newer section that I entered the church. After I was clicked through, I walked toward voices I heard chatting softly and found myself in a small room with three people engaged in quiet office activities. The back wall held numerous screens receiving live feed from what must have been dozens of security cameras aimed at exterior and interior landscapes of the church. With just one quick glance at all those screens, I had a visual access to all the secrets within and without the building.

I was so distracted by the screens with their blinking perspective changes that I forgot I was a guest in a church with three people staring at me. The room fell silent. I felt like a doctor examining their x-rays, exposing their innards without an invitation to do so. Just as I was about to break my gaze from all those screens, two things happened. First, I recognized Simeon in one of the frames. He was probably just moving closer to the building to get a picture for my records, but on that grainy, black-and-white screen he looked like he was creeping about the premises, his big camera snapping shots through the tinted windows. Second, a man came rushing into the room, interrupting the silence with, "There's a man out there with a camera . . ." He didn't finish his sentence because he suddenly recognized that there was a stranger among them. I was happy to have interrupted his thought in that the first part of his sentence was so intense and full of alarm that he could have easily finished it with, "Grab your gun, David, we're going after him."

He froze when he saw me and tried to connect the dots with a stranger in the office and the intruder on his front lawn guilelessly taking photos. I was mainly embarrassed for Simeon to be caught on the film that we all now stood watching, but I also felt amused by the situation. Simeon took his time, as is his way, focusing, checking the camera settings, focusing again. We watched him in silence until I said quietly, "That's my husband," knowing it wouldn't answer any of their questions but may move us past this awkward part.

"Who are you?" asked the man who turned out to be David Eggelston, First Baptist Church's choir director. I reached out my hand and feared for a blink or so that he would reach back and put me in cuffs. The others were still watching Simeon walk around on their grass, taking random pictures from different angles. I sent him a telepathic message to *retreat, drive away, save yourself,* but his receptors were defective as evidenced on the screen showing his ceaseless clicking of the camera.

"I'm Abigail," I offered, shaking David's hand. "I'm writing a book about Mario McNeill." I could tell instantly that this was a big mistake, the exact opposite of what they wanted to hear.

First of all, I was not writing a book about McNeill, and so I broke the ninth commandment standing inside, indeed *locked* inside, sacred real estate. Second, I knew from my research that Reverend Birch was a member of the clergy there and that he knew McNeill. But I did not know his standing among the church staff. Having been intimately involved in a church myself, I knew there can be certain quirky staff members who are enfolded into leadership more as an act of ministry itself than any meaningful appointment. Church draws out the freaks, which was apparently the way Jesus wanted it when he wandered around befriending misanthropic fishermen and cheating tax collectors. Judging from my small audience's reaction to the McNeill name, I could not eliminate the possibility that Birch was among in leadership and that the church proper would prefer to disassociate from both characters.

When I blurted out that I was writing a book about McNeill, my husband's actions with the camera became insignificant as all four people turned to stare at me. They didn't project menace as much as malice. Although I knew instantly I had said the wrong thing, I didn't know *why* it was the wrong thing, so it was going to be tricky to try to fix it. "It's a book about forgiveness." I added. I'm not certain why I added that bit, maybe because I was locked in a labyrinth of a church and I needed theirs. The words softened the church folk so I kept tiptoeing in that direction. "Yeah," I continued extemporaneously now, "I want to explore the idea of forgiveness despite the magnitude of the offense." They kept listening so I kept talking, and the longer I spoke, the more they relaxed. I was horrified by what was coming out, things like, and "Mario was a young boy once, with promise and hope." While this was true, I had no intention of discussing it in my book. I remember seeing Simeon walk out of the security camera's range, and I prayed he was darting to the car and wasn't going to reappear up on the surveillance camera housed on the roof. I wouldn't put it past him; he's dogged with things like this. I told David that I was looking for Reverend Birch, and at the mention of his name, the whole group collectively exhaled and even the video surveillance looked less strained.

They all knew McNeill, of course. There weren't many people in Fayetteville or its surrounding areas who weren't familiar with the triad nomenclature of Mario/Shaniya/Antoinette. The three names had melded into one through the heat of the crime and the combination of their roles in it. It's possible the church staff were relieved because they realized they wouldn't be required to come up with a sound byte for the evening news. They could slough it off to Reverend Birch.

Although I am not a member of the press, I usually find it helpful to associate myself with press writers when investigating a story. In normal circumstances, people seem eager to have their words written down and published. But this was decidedly not the case in Fayetteville. I frequently had to reassure people that I was *not* with the press. Fayetteville citizens felt harassed and exposed by the national press vans that overtook their city—first, when Shaniya was reported missing, and then again, four years later when McNeill and Davis were brought to trial. They didn't like the press, and even the mention of *McNeill's* or *Davis'* name brought about an instant antagonism.

But these were Christians and I was a guest in their house. They treated my questions with a careful hospitality, but once they realized I was looking for Birch, they offered me his information in such detail, I feared they would reveal the man's personal habits. They were quite eager to help me on my way, and if they could hand deliver me to Birch, all the better for them. David walked me to the door where he had to use a keycard to let me out. I certainly hoped they used less restrictive measures on Sunday mornings. I asked if Mario was a member of their church, and again, they looked relieved. David, who was now the spokesperson for the little group, laughed and answered, "No, no. Mario never came to church here." I was puzzled, wondering how Birch was thrust into the position of damage control at his trial. David answered my unasked question, "His mother, Juanita Ball, is a member here. She actually works in the office." I quickly turned to examine the two women standing in our little group who had not yet spoken. They immediately found industry in another room.

"How does Reverend Birch know Mario?" I asked.

"Oh, well," David said as he swiped his card to allow my exit, "you'll have to speak to Reverend Birch about that."

I ejected myself from the church and sprinted to the car where Simeon sat examining his pictures, completely unaware that his actions had all been documented and viewed in real time. "How did it go in there?" he asked me cheerfully.

"Best just to drive away," I said. "I got what I needed." And this was true. I received information that would push my research forward. But I also received something I didn't expect. I watched those humble, church staff members rallying around each other at the hint of threat against their group. The son of one of their dedicated parishioners was sitting on death row for the rape and murder of a young girl, and they gathered around him like the Christians gathered around one another in the coliseums when pitted against the lions. In this arena, I was the predator and McNeill needed protection. Amid the flood of mortal ills prevailing, the church stood as a mighty fortress, a bulwark to protect one of their own.

> *. . . there really are no words to describe this mother. She doesn't even deserve the compliment of "mother." Her and her cohorts' animalistic behavior screams out for the North Carolina death penalty.*
> – CNN transcript from the *Nancy Grace* show, November 17, 2009

Sentencing

ANTOINETTE AND HER sisters had been assisted by a neighborhood connection not unlike McNeill's church. It was an observant neighbor who called DSS, an eyewitness to Priscilla's erratic drug behavior and its effects on her girls. DSS swept in and removed her and her sisters. DSS was commissioned to move them into competent care, but due to multiple failings within the organization, they had simply moved them to their grandmother's house, a place their mother was free to enter at any time. This neighbor who called was a friend of her mother and, according to Antoinette, "knew what was going on." What was going on was negligent and criminal. This woman's phone call had the power to alter the course of Antoinette's life. Had DSS accomplished its mission of protection and care, it's doubtful that a 14-year-old Antoinette would have watched as her 20-year-old boyfriend was given permission to move in with her family. His endorsed residency resulted in a pregnancy by the time Antoinette was 15.

Had she not become a teenage mother, she would have had no reason to begin stripping to make money. She could have enjoyed the rest of her high school years, continuing in her ROTC program, which she loved. Antoinette had her sights on a career in the Navy. Under a capable and educated guardian, Antoinette may have had a chance to escape many of the systematic bindings placed around her life, securing her to a course predetermined by her mother and her mother's mother ad nauseum.

Such was the evidence against Antoinette, including a signed confession. Her attorneys chose to make a plea deal rather than subject her to the possible three life sentences that the jury could have handed down. That Antoinette was guilty of her crimes is an arguable conclusion. But the walk she had taken to reach the courtroom on the day of her sentencing had been a long one. Was it, perhaps, an inevitable one as well? When the nation watched Antoinette walk into the courtroom for her sentencing, they saw a broken woman, shackled and chained. "Lock her up forever," the public shouted, not understanding that she was shackled long before she arrived at that courtroom. The sentence for her life was passed decades before The Honorable Judge Ammons made it official.

Sanitation

SHANIYA'S BODY WAS taken out of the wilderness and transported to the county coroner's office where Dr. Thomas Clark examined her for cause of death. Her body was so deeply decomposed that she arrived at his office in two separate body bags. It is a biting irony that it would be the circumstance of her death that would lead Shaniya to be delivered into able and capable hands for the first time in her life. Dr. Clark was a certified forensic pathologist with twenty years' experience in the North Carolina medical examiner's office. He served as its deputy chief medical examiner for eight of those twenty years. He is a soft-spoken man, thoughtful and careful in his deliveries. When he testified, four years after he examined Shaniya's body, the courtroom sat in silence as he gently delivered the brutal details of the little girl's death and postmortem treatment.

Clark, along with his North Carolina colleagues, performed about 1,300 autopsies that year in addition to reviewing thousands of others, which spoke to his ethos on the stand. But even with all of his experience, the condition of Shaniya's body was too broken down to be of any definitive use. Clark estimated that her body had been "in the elements at least six days." These were no ordinary days. It was a wet, cold November that year, with the average temperature just fifty-six degrees during her six days lying exposed among scrub oaks and kudzu. But he was able to identify the manner of death: asphyxiation. Additionally, he was able to determine in his examination that Shaniya had "injuries to her vagina that were highly likely to have been caused before death." His final analysis was a definitive diagnosis that Shaniya was raped at or around, but not after her murder.

The police detectives, through an analysis of McNeill's geographic timeline and by observing his choice of locations, determined that his thirty-eight minutes spent in room 201 of the Comfort Inn confirmed Dr. Clark's autopsy findings. All the professionals in the field agreed on this point. But their belief would not be enough to convict McNeill of rape. The forensics would be against them. First, Shaniya's body was so badly decomposed that Clark was unable to determine any genetic contributors—foreign DNA—found in or around her vagina. This means that he was unable to label or identify any semen on her body. This left investigators with only the scene of the crime for forensic evidence, and it was this hotel room that would cause their charge to fail as a conviction. Despite meritorious efforts to lift McNeill's or Shaniya's DNA from the hotel bedspread, their attempts were unsuccessful.

This failure might speak more to the filth of the comforter itself than to results of the testing. The Fayetteville Police Department forensic lab testified that the hotel comforter contained too many contributing specimens (DNA from prior guests) to provide any possibility of a firm match. Because the more pressing issue at the time of the results was to solve the mystery of Shaniya's last hours, there was no indictment against the Comfort Inn for crimes against human decency by allowing such contaminated bedding into any hotel room. The hotel's oversight of basic hygienic standards would allow McNeill to be found "not guilty" on the charge of rape. The jury believed he committed the rape, but the evidence, because it was diluted and indeterminate, allowed for the legal status of "reasonable doubt."

The Dunce Cap

ABOUT THE TIME Antoinette started a service job at the Carolina Inn, I found a job as an assistant innkeeper, which I hated, but started grad school, which I loved. The latter would prove to be a short-lived love affair, but I maintained my hate for the inn-keeping job for the entire six months I labored there.

I had earned my undergraduate degree and felt steady enough in flight to increase my mileage for a master's degree. I had packed up my chicks and with my beloved books in tow, moved to Asheville, North Carolina.

Jan and Harvey, the proprietors of the bed and breakfast I worked for, served their hospitality with a generous measure of bitterness. Even as a newcomer to their home, I could read the faded wallpaper clearly enough to see that they were a couple who should have retired years ago–or perhaps never stepped into the hospitality business in the first place. Both of their faces boasted an identical pinched forehead that betrayed their large, but careful smiles.

Jan was in charge of the training, and we sat together in the pleasant sunroom with manuals and notebooks stacked between us full of information about the inn.

She was very organized about the training, and, had I been less desperate for employment, I would have interpreted her high skill level as having a direct correlation to her high turnover rate, which would have pointed to a difficult work environment. But, in the beginning, I counted myself lucky to have landed on their impressive stone porch on the heels of the departure of the former assistant innkeeper Bonnie. According to Jan, Bonnie was, "a dedicated dunce." As we slowly turned the pages in those giant three-ring binders, Jan offered anecdotal evidence to each training component demonstrating Bonnie's, or before her, Jackie's incompetence. *Offer the guests a tour of the inn upon their arrival. Refer to the History of the Inn Binder for details,* the manual instructed. Jan leaned in after reading the caption as if offering a confession, "Bonnie once told a guest that we had actual shell casings embedded in the staircase from the Civil War," she chortled. "What a darling little dolt she was!" She pushed her glasses back up to the bridge of her nose and commenced reading. Jan read each section out loud, which is as useful an education as reading the nutrition label on a box without being told what's inside. She broke down the requirements of the inn into microscopic tasks, causing me to become confused about my main job.

What kind of product was I: the waitress for the three-course breakfast, the dishwasher or the front face of the company? I never understood who they wanted me to be because every task, from sweeping the dining room floor to ordering supplies to accepting payments, had lengthy sections and sometimes subsections of procedural steps in their bundle of manuals. Jan was naturally suspicious of *outsiders*, a term that included all her guests, her entire employee staff and, on occasion, her husband Harvey. She shifted her suspicion about me between the two scales of *absolute moron* and *conspiring to steal something from me*. By the end of my six-month sentence there, I was guilty of both crimes.

Harvey approached his role with the expectation that his expectations would never be met. Like Glen back at 4766 Hurless Drive, he was a man driven by a complicated and detailed system of repetition. And like Glen, Harvey's detailed attention focused on anything financial. Jan managed and ran every minutia of the three-story house with the notable exception of the kitchen. This was Harvey's domain. Like Jan, Harvey, being a man driven by control and procedure, alternated between two unwavering menus at breakfast. For example: Saturday morning I served pecan-encrusted French toast with peppery bacon and the Sunday morning table always, always saw German eggs with spiced apples. Despite an enticing and comprehensive recipe section on their website, Harvey was a stickler for predictability. The eggs would never be served with bacon because in his world, they made no sense without the French toast. Harvey was a micromanager.

While Jan poured hours of effort into training, Harvey spent hours following me around that little kitchen, watching carefully for my mistakes. Some days he wasn't able to find any during my actual shift, but I could count on finding little, yellow sticky notes the next day. I arrived several hours before him, and the first time I unlocked the back door (for servants), I thought he was playing a practical joke with the sticky notes that decorated multiple items in the kitchen. But, after reading the indictments—*this creamer belongs in dining room cupboard, not kitchen; towels must be hung on the rack above the desk, not on the oven handle; noticed several water spots on the knives, you must pay closer attention*—I understood two things: one, Jan and Harvey didn't joke, and two, this job was going to be tiresome.

They were obsessed with saving money, and their worry over the pennies left me hand-wringing each week that they might not make payroll. Harvey insisted that I re-use the little butter pat left by each plate on French Toast Day. In the beginning, I protested, citing sanitation concerns and pointing out that a miserly attitude seemed counterproductive in the hospitality industry. But Harvey was insistent and because my heart raced at the thought of a sticky note the next morning, I obliged. Each Saturday morning during clean-up, I dutifully collected the little dishes of personal butter pats, even the ones that had their little corners cut off and used, and stored them for their second run the next morning. Every time I heard a guest sneeze at the table or heard someone speak with food in his mouth while I served coffee, I imagined all those germs gravitating to those recycled butter pats and shuddered. Like many of the products they served, I stuck with the job way past my shelf date. Despite my stomach burning each time I turned the key in that back-door lock, I remained loyal to Jan and Harvey for reasons I can't fully understand.

I knew they were speaking poorly of me to Harvey's sister, who frequently called the inn. Jan had a little office up in the eave of the kitchen where she could watch over her kingdom as if from a throne. She sat up there chatting away to her sister-in-law, offering open commentary about my current task performance or detailing my latest transgression. She spoke to me through the sister-in-law, and I found her tactics dishonorable. "Abigail thinks I don't know that she threw an extra handful of chocolate chips into the batter for the guest's afternoon cookies, but I measure the inventory." She spoke loudly from her cramped loft, implying that her message was for the caller but intending it for me. My cheeks grew hot, but instead of confronting her, I scrubbed a clean pot or waxed the floor in an attempt to win her approval. Because I am a people pleaser, I remained in constant motion, attempting to please two people who managed to live their lives in a condition of chronic disapproval.

The three of us bristled and bucked up against each other until the day I made a mistake that no sticky note, not even a pink one reserved for more serious offenses, could cover. I secured my place as the "most doltish of the dunces" and knew my transgression would be passed down in the sunroom from assistant innkeeper to assistant innkeeper until Jan and Harvey lay pinched in their graves, perhaps next to their koi pond full of fish that I fed from a carefully measured scoop of dog food each day. And even then my mistake may live on in the very walls of the old house that may or may not have held Civil War relics within its ancient wood.

It was a bustling Sunday morning (German eggs and spiced apples) with many guests needing directions to this or that attraction in our little mountain town. I was always nervous about giving directions because I was new to town and unsure myself. I also had a time clock ticking in the back of my brain; each second that passed punctuated a bulleted task from one of the big procedural manuals. I was required to perform each task within a certain period of time. And so pesky questions from chatty guests always increased my heart rate and usually secured some oversight on my part. They all clustered around me after breakfast, and I itemized the chores relating to the table clean-up in my head as they sought my attention. One woman, who was housed in the discounted third-floor bedroom, complained that her whirlpool needed cleaning out before she returned back from her excursion.

This sent me into a panic. The whirlpools were not scheduled to be cleaned until Monday after check-out. Jan would not be happy with this change in routine. Adding to my distress was the fact that Jan was breaking in a new housekeeper. She was a younger girl, probably just turned 18. She was sweet and shy and likely chosen for the job because she could easily be molded into a working machine. I asked her if she would add the third-floor whirlpool to her own chore list that day. She told me that she had not been trained on the procedure for cleaning out whirlpools. Even in her naïveté, she recognized that, above all, the manuals must be followed. Whirlpool cleaning was beyond the scope of my job descriptions and so, when I secured a free minute, I quickly called Jan for instruction to this intrusion in the line-up of tasks that remained undone.

She assured me that "even a simpleton" could do the job, which I took as her endorsement of my qualifications. She proceeded to explain to me, in manual style, how to fill, chemicalize and scrub the whirlpool. I was sweating just listening to her. A few guests were still hanging onto my skirts, needing attention like stray children, and the breakfast table was not yet cleared. Jan kept talking, detailing the job and speaking slowly to accommodate my stupidity as I stared at the butter pats absorbing all of the germs that flew through the air. Jan finally felt she had conveyed the job, after I assured her multiple times that I was up to the task.

I rolled my eyes as I hung up the phone, frustrated at her impression of my incompetence. I assisted the remaining guests and then zipped up to the third floor to start the procedure. It was one of the inn's tasks that was time consuming and multi-stepped. I filled the tub with water, watching it slowly creep up past the rubber spray jets, worrying over all of my unattended chores down below. Once it reached this mark, I obeyed Jan by not letting it "go one drop past the sprayers" and put in the chemical, turned off the faucet and started the jets. I watched the water dance about for a few minutes longer, then ran back down to the main floor to tackle the breakfast cleanup.

Their dishwasher was on some sort of automatic lock that would prohibit me from opening it if I didn't get the dishes in on time. Then I would be stuck washing them by hand, and this always created a cavalcade of sticky notes the next day. I cleared the table in record speed and, to save time, tossed all the butter pats into the bin, careful to cover them with the empty egg cartons in case there was an investigation. I had just finished the dishes when I heard a guest fiddling about in the entrance hall. I walked out to her while drying my hands on my apron. She stood underneath a grand light fixture, prisms of glass hanging from the featured chandelier. She had forgotten which way to turn at the main road and had come back for more detailed instruction.

Because I had beaten the dishwasher, I felt comfortable offering her more generous attention. She was one of those slow, Southern talkers, taking her time with the syllables, stretching out her vowels while touching my arm for emphasis. It was just after one of these arm touches that I felt the first drop of water fall onto my head. It confused me, as I tried to relate it to the woman and her tactile habit. Suddenly, I felt another drop; this one hit the front of my forehead and began slowly dripping down my nose before falling to the floor between us. She stopped talking as we both lifted our chins in slow motion to the ceiling. In horror, I saw that globed chandelier filling with water that was now running rather than dripping out of the light fixture. A little scream escaped my throat as I attacked the staircase two steps at a time. I arrived at the tippy-top third floor and fumbled with the keys to get into the room. Once I had it unlocked, I held the handle for half a second before turning it, willing the water from the whirlpool to be happily dancing about inside the tub.

When I turned the knob and entered the room, the floor already was an inch thick in water. I sopped my way over to the tub, looking around the infrastructure for the leak. There was none. I grew more desperate, falling to my knees, trying to find how the water was escaping onto the floor and through two ceilings, making its way down to that landing floor chandelier. I was close to hyperventilating as I ran my hands along the outside of the tub, feeling for the hole like a blind woman. My skirt was now soaked, and still the water kept splashing. It was then that I understood it was spilling out from the top of the tub. But how could this be? Precious minutes ticked by as I attempted to figure out the problem. No water was pouring from the faucet. I had turned that off before I raced downstairs to compete against the timer on the dishwasher.

I plunged an arm into the tub, my hair falling into the bleached water, and let up the plug. The water drained slowly out, taking its time as it lazily snaked its way down the drain. I was still on my hands and knees, completely soaked by now, when I saw my mistake. I had shut off the water that led to a fancy faucet over the tub. But there was a second water source, hidden among the jets. It still flooded into the tub at full force. I hadn't shut off the source, just one of its outlets. I grabbed the bath towels hanging on the hooks to sop up the water, but it was much like using a BAND-AID to mend a severed artery. I pulled the bedspread off the bed, and it quickly saturated. I was desperately grabbing at the sheets when the cook came up to inspect my distress. He was a petty man, unpleasant in every way but most especially in hygiene. He never forgave me for telling Harvey that he took the unused muffins from breakfast home for his dog Salamander. Although we didn't re-use those (to my knowledge), Harvey was furious, feeling that something had been stolen from him. Harvey took to skulking around the kitchen while the cook sweated over the hot griddle, glaring at me over the steamy heat of the iron. I came to dread the weekend breakfast service because the cook went out of his way to make me look stupid in front of Jan or Harvey. He needn't have tried so hard; he was performing for an audience who already believed his premise to be true.

The cook stood over me as I futilely attempted to absorb the water, but we both knew that the damage was done. "I've called Harvey," he sneered on his way out the door. I willed him to slip in the water and break his cocky nose, but I heard him clump down the staircase in triumph. Harvey and Jan arrived shortly after, but even with their dehumidifiers and clipped commands that were meant to convey judgment—"strip the sheets from the second floor bedroom; they are soaking the mattress and we can't afford to replace it"—we all were waiting for the inevitable.

After the initial frantic industry of triage, we all settled ourselves into twelve hours of mopping, stripping, fanning and drying. At the end of the day, Jan sat me down and asked what went wrong. Such was the level of her dismay that her normally boisterous voice was low and shaky. "How did this happen?" she asked, and for the first time since we met, I saw her as small and scared.

I answered with the only possible option, "I made a mistake." She shook her head, more disappointed in herself for not recognizing the profound level of my ineptitude than at my admission. I resigned right then, sitting there wet and exhausted in front of her. She refused my resignation but agreed to take away my wages for the day to help offset the costs.

The next day the second- and first-floor ceilings collapsed, causing the whole business to shut down for the entire week. Jan asked me to work through the end of the tourist season, which was in two months' time. I don't know why she asked me to stay; perhaps she felt she owned a piece of me then. I felt so guilty about the damage to the inn and how expensive it was all going to be that I agreed to stay on. My tail remained between my legs all fifty-two days I worked for them. Each day felt like a slow-motion trip to the dentist chair to have a tooth pulled.

But during my penance, the inn offered me a respite. At night, when all the guests were out to dinner and my chores were finished, I hushed the prohibitive voices of Jan and Harvey that I carried in my head and crept out from my stool in the kitchen. I nestled myself in the massive leather sofa in the grand salon and read crime stories.

Do you really think that you will show a similarity between the readers and myself, as well as yourself? Because I don't. You're a professor and going by statistics, I doubt very much that my life and your life have any similarities.
– Antoinette Davis in a letter, April 6, 2015

BTU

I READ OVER Antoinette Davis' list of convictions. Their weight depressed me. I knew enough from my informal association with the legal system—meaning I watched a lot of *Dateline*—to know that the prosecutor stacks charges, hoping the collective weight will crush the defendant. And this list was crushing. It was odd that her "Primary Offense" was "Sex Offense with a Child by an Adult." This crime is gruesome, no question, but further down the list, almost buried as an afterthought, was the "Murder in the Second Degree."

Murder is a nuanced word. At first glance it appears to present itself straightforwardly: a person is alive and then another person intervenes and causes her death. Simple. There is a bad guy and a victim.

But murder is murky. It is not simple. To see it as the death of something—a belief, a dream, a relationship—at the hands of someone else is to recognize that no human has a special immunity from devastating damage or grief. Each one of us carries a story of betrayal and some form of murder written into our life's narrative. We are all both murderers and murdered.

Back when I was married to my first husband, years before he announced his proclivity of sexual attraction to men, he attempted to educate me on the Christian Culture. Our marriage would require me to join his church and, like the poor widowed Old Testament Ruth, to call his people my people. Our wedding date approaching, he was heavily into the planning of the event. At the time, I didn't find his intense discussions concerning our china pattern or his detailed worry over the cardstock used for the invitations as having any meaning at all aside from his flamboyant personality.

I was happy to let him concern himself over the floral arrangements ("I must have a gardenia for my button hole") or the seating chart for the dinner ("Gee, Mamma's like to come up from the grave like Lazarus if we put cousin JoJo at the head table next to Uncle Hee-Haw"). Southerners rally around their nicknames. Jeff's Georgia family was full of such endearments, "Bow-Bow," "Lil' Freddy," "Boo-Bear" among them. I frequently confused the pets' names with the owners'. Did Sugar own Trixie or was it the other way around? When the nicknamed person brought shame to the family, epithets replaced nicknames. After one scandal, the more loquacious members declared, "That Tramp Donna had a baby without the benefit of nuptials!" For as long as I had known the family, *that tramp* was irrevocably attached to Donna. Later, as I considered Jeff's pronouncements on Christian judgment and forgiveness, the expression returned to me with force. Through our courtship I studied his Southern family, watching them strip their field peas on the front porch, set their tomato aspics and maul their neighbor's misfortunes while serving them ambrosia on a pretty flowered plate after Sunday service.

At the time, I had little interest in the peculiarities of Christian morality and simply accepted that Jeff's status as Christian pushed the possibilities of a baby before our ceremony into the miracle category. I let Jeff's excitement over wedding planning relax my own self-judgments at my indifference toward it. Years later, after all those late-night Internet liaisons in chat rooms with gay men using very different sorts of nicknames like "Bulging College Boy" or "Muscle Mack Smack," his wedding day hysteria about the candles dripping onto the silver platters made more sense.

Back when I was swept along by the steady current of social expectations, I allowed him to paddle my boat straight to the matrimonial altar because this sanctified mooring was where I was expected to arrive. My own twin sister, after all, had been married nearly five years and had already produced two offspring. I was almost 30, and the questioning looks, implying "shouldn't you be married by now?" frequently shadowed my path. Our marriage was the result of propulsion and compulsion. I felt propelled by the current of social acceptance, and he felt compelled by an undercurrent of desire not to be gay. For very different reasons, we both believed we needed the marriage, but what we tried to navigate together was not navigable. It was not marriage; it was cover against the elements. He covered my need to look normal, and I covered his need to look straight. Our wedding portrait showed a buoyantly smiling, connected couple, but once life itself, with the babies and the poverty, scratched the paint off our canvas, the sketch beneath revealed two people drowning—who should not, under any circumstances, however noble they may appear, be married.

But during our courtship, back when our smiles were strong enough to mask the strain behind them, my fiancé attempted to teach me how to become a Christian wife. Like him, I had grown up in a church-on-Sunday-mornings-and-Wednesday-nights Christian home. My father Glen's own father had been a founding member of the Perry Christian Church congregation that my childhood family all attended. Our mom, Caroline, got up early every Sunday morning to sear a pot roast in butter before adding carrots and potatoes, plopping down the heavy metal lid and turning the range to "simmer through the sermon." She did this every Sunday without exception, and when she walked out years later, my sister and I slipped unnoticed into her rhythm, performing the task just as she had, allowing all of us to pretend that she had never left, or perhaps that she had never been there at all.

Through all those years of pot roasts and Sunday morning sermons, the directives of our father were calm but far from subtle. He had an intense interest in British Thermal Units (BTUs) and created elaborate charts to track their use and waste. He pulled into the gravel driveway punctually at twenty minutes past five every day, grabbed his clipboard he had attached to the garage wall and walked around to the back of the house to log the numbers found on the electrical meter. The climate of the rest of the evening depended on the outcome of these numbers. If they were too high, there would be solemn punishments. In the sixteen years I lived in his house, I never knew the numbers to come in too low. He had all manner of tricks and tips to keep these numbers low. We all learned to grow panicked over an escaped BTU. "Close that refrigerator door!" he would quietly command, "The BTUs are escaping." It was the same for light bulbs and open external doors. He developed a protocol to keep the BTUs trapped inside. The refrigerator was allowed to be open twice a day: Once to prepare dinner, then again to clean up. The lights were not to be turned on under any circumstance until dusk. He even went through a toilet-flushing phase when he instructed us to flush once a day before bed. Years later, after my own daring escape in which I allowed as many BTUs to get out with me as I could by leaving my bedroom window open in the winter, I read about Anne Frank and her pre-captive captivity in the warehouse attic. Like my brother and sister, Anne and her sibling were permitted to flush the toilet once a day, lest the workers down in the warehouse hear the water running through the pipes and discover those hidden upstairs. In my own captivity, the flushing of the toilet or the lurking about in a dark house had less to do with discovery and more to do with liability. Each action was attached to a master budget that placed it on the asset or liability side. My sister and I entered into the master budget on the liability side due to our gender. No matter how many lightbulbs we kept off or how fast we closed the refrigerator door each day, we could never repay the debt we incurred through our "It's a girl, it's another girl" birth. I never understood the complexities of BTUs, but I most certainly understood their driven, determined desire to escape.

Our father, a church deacon and then later an elder, guided his family ship with precision and detailed attention. In addition to his reverence for the patriarchy of the Christian belief system itself, Glen's own moral compass informed the direction of his leadership. Found in the central organ of his body, that compass pointed him in the right direction. Some of his organ reverence came to him honestly. His family considered it deeply unlucky to be born a female. An unlucky double-X stroke of bad fortune. Caroline likely felt doubly doomed from the start of her pregnancy when she discovered she was carrying female twins.

Frenetic panic—such as occurred, for instance, when the pastor came to the house on the eve of our baptisms—ran under the surface of a daily ritual that Glen kept under his deliberate, quiet control. He ran his home with a steady, dependable routine, one that rarely saw visitors.

It wasn't just a pot roast Sunday. It was a Wednesday night hamburger noodle casserole and Thursday night hot dogs with potato chips. There was a meal to go with every night. Glen presided over these suppers and over all of the goings out and comings in. Like God running Perry Christian Church, Glen ran 4766 Hurless Drive with both omnipresence and omnipotence. We were all trained to behave quietly and without fanfare or fuss. In the sixteen years I lived in his house, I only knew Glen to lose control of his domain one time. My sister, for reasons that still remain unclear—though perhaps not without emblematic significance of the kind that can sometimes be assigned in retrospect—depressed the sink sprayer with tape so it would spray water on Glen's clothes when he washed his hands before dinner. Even then, he emitted only a tiny, almost whispered "oh," barely audible from our hiding place in the broom closet around the corner. With that one exception, he kept to his deliberate, quiet control.

Beneath the placid lake that was 4766 Hurless Drive, however, there raged a maelstrom of harm that released its grip only when we were in public. School became our shelter during the week and Sunday mornings our one refuge during those long weekends. At school and at church, we were permitted to surface from the ongoing drowning of our childhood to catch our breath and see the sights above the murky, cold depths.

As I came of age, I left the church, confused by a God who ran a Red Cross center in the middle of my war. Every Sunday and every Wednesday I would approach his altar for the blood transfusion that the Christians called communion. "This is my blood, take and drink." And I drank and I drank, willing his blood to transfuse my own. I was a Jet Cadet for Jesus. I was a soldier for the Lord. Every week God and his church staff patched me up and sent me back to the front lines. I was on God's cosmic conveyor belt that ran from the tent of the holy of holies where I would be sanctified, out the back flap to Hurless Drive where I would be shamed. Survival in Glen's house required an untiring hypervigilance beyond any reasonable human ability, even for a well-trained soldier like me. Sometimes our genius brother would stand sentry with a hoarse whisper in the hallway—"He's in there," nodding toward Glen's bedchamber, "Get outside and play." Or, on the Sunday night living room gathering to watch *Hee-Haw* (popcorn for the kids, Royal Gold Pretzel Sticks for Glen), "Those shorts are too short; go change into long pants; otherwise, he'll just stare the whole time." But even our brother's tireless efforts were not strong enough to create a safe harbor. At night, in our double bed, my sister and I scootched as close as we could to each other, saving a tiny space in the middle for Jesus. He was meant to serve as our protector. We were taught to see Jesus as a gentle lamb, but our circumstances required us to use a bit of literary license. Our Jesus was more of a badass bouncer. But even Jesus couldn't help us on nights when Glen's determined footsteps triggered the hallway floorboards to send us a warning message which we acutely received, a message that left us only a few seconds of disoriented decision making. The girl closest to the door would be tagged as "it." Should we trade places? Who went the last time? One girl would be required to accompany him across the hall while the other would remain in bed, tossing between the two anchors of relief and guilt.

In my adult life, I clung to the reason and logic of education, scorning the faith of the little children. It was better for me to believe in no God at all than to believe in a God who ran his kingdom like a capitalist, supplying the pain for free, and then charging a lifetime of servitude for the cure. Even all these years later, with so much geography and time between Hurless Drive and my own home, school remains the place where I feel I can inhale properly. I became a college instructor mainly to supply my body with the life-giving oxygen I have always felt was amply stored within the classrooms and hallways.

Divorcing God

I WAS OVER 40 when I graduated with my Bachelor's degree. I attempted college directly out of high school but was politely academically dismissed at the end of my freshman year. Dean Oosting called me to his office and appeared quite pained to inform me that my invitation to their school had been revoked. He seemed genuinely depressed, both at my carelessness with their educational opportunity and at his task of imparting the bad news. "You can do better than this," he told me as he handed me the official copy of my dismissal. I tried to take the confirmation of my failure from his long, elegant hand, but he repeated his statement before he let go. "You can do better than this."

At the time, standing there in his office with the blue carpet and bright, happy windows, I felt worse for him than I did for myself. In my personal failings, I had somehow injured him. Because I lacked any direction or even a modicum of ambition, I hung around the small campus for another semester, working in the cafeteria line as the food dumper. As the trays came back to the kitchen from a small conveyor belt, my job was to swipe the remaining food into large trash bins and then line the trays up for the industrial dishwasher to clean. It was a humble job and one that I believed likely represented my future prospects. It was my personal version of serving fries to those more deserving. But the job kept me connected to my friends on campus and allowed me to keep my academic dismissal a secret. I lived the shadow life of a fake student. The kids on campus assumed I was still a student as I waved my gloved hand at them through the little window as they handed me their used plates. But close to the middle of the semester, I was finally exposed as an imposter.

One day, Pat Baumgardner, a particularly plain but popular girl, called to me through the little window that separated the workers from the WASPs. "Hey, Abigail, I heard you got kicked out of school." She didn't say it loudly, but rather dropped her voice, making her words more enticing and juicy. There were only a few other kids standing nearby, but that's all it took. They looked at me through the window and saw a failure wearing rubber gloves and a giant rubber apron, scraping their discarded garbage into a big bin. I saw myself through their eyes, and that image served as a freeze-frame for the next two decades of my life.

I eventually worked as a waitress off campus. But the next long years became an endless, tiresome parade of rubber-glove jobs performed in the back of a pretty building. The buildings and the cities changed with time, but the jobs remained identical. Later, I married and had three children, but even then, standing at my own kitchen sink, scraping used food from dirty plates, I felt the Pats of the world, watching me through my window and calling me out as an imposter. And they were right. My life had become a con job with me deceiving everyone that I was a good mother or a dutiful wife or a loving servant of God. I had everyone but myself convinced that I was an exceptional human.

I would sometimes catch my reflection in a glass window, and we would knowingly nod to each other, acknowledging the farce that was my life. "You can do better than this," we'd tell each other.

When I finally wrenched myself from the servitude of marriage and missionary work, I began work at a boutique potato chip company in Atlanta and went back to school. I stuffed my three children and myself into a tiny condo and set about the business of creating a new life. That is how I saw it at the time; I was starting a new life with no religious or marital restrictions. But looking back from the vantage point of time, I see it now as less a definition and more a reclaiming. This was not a renovation but a restoration. I remembered who I was. For the first time since crawling out my childhood window at 4766 Hurless Drive, I stopped running.

I graduated from Georgia State University three years later and marched with thousands of others into the arena, our tassels bouncing with each proud step. Because the school was so large, they had to streamline the graduation process, perfecting an ingenious system of processing huge herds of cattle while still making each sow or bull feel accomplished. We could not walk across a stage to hear our names individually called, but, instead stood up in a large clump of graduates when our discipline was called. "School of Education," the announcer echoed into the cavernous hall and a couple hundred students rose from their metal folding chairs and received a group commencement. Family and friends cheered from the faraway stands.

"School of Arts and Sciences" boomed out from the speakers, and I stood with four thousand others. I watched my children way up in the bleachers jump up and down screaming and waving their happiness at me. It was my most defining moment as a parent and it remains an ironic twist that my now adult children see my school years as ones stolen from them.

I see all those years in the ministry spent in poverty, gasping under the endless workload of service to the poor and service to my children, calculating a judicious way to split an apple among twelve people as stolen from them. But my children saw the triumph of my schooling as selfish. What they do not yet know is that every hour I spent washing a prostitute's hair, cleaning up her vomit from my bathroom floor, praying and worshiping in a tiny living room for hours and hours, each time pushing my children to the side, that *this* was my failing. This was my selfishness. I elevated the "lowest of the low" above my children, above myself. This is my crime. I walked through my own life like a zombie-vampire, sucking blood from those in my path to keep myself alive. The more I consumed, the more robust I became. "Abigail is such a sacrificial Christian," the Pat Baumgardners now whispered. "She gives up everything for the poor. What a shining example to her children!" And while I masqueraded as a doting mother and decent human, I knew my insides were rotten. I used the poor and I used my own children for self-elevation. Because my actions had been endorsed by God, I made it look honorable and praiseworthy. But it was abject selfishness. Every, "You give so much," or "You're an amazing woman of God" fueled my ego tank and energized me to serve longer and sacrifice louder.

Even without the missionary work to tip my life into a more saintly light, I lived my more pedestrian roles as a mother and a wife because I felt it was my duty. And I found ways to convert my enduring commitment to this duty into sacrificial glory as well. I birthed three children in four years, served the poor by joining their ranks and transported my children multiple times back and forth across the globe, once all the way to Hong Kong, all the while strapping a baby to my back so my hands were free to serve the poor. The more difficult the task, the more delicious the prize.

The kids finally grew old enough to be in school, and this offered me more time to dedicate to service until, finally, everything became too noisy. We had moved to London by then, wanting to expand our service to an international level. That's what we said on our monthly newsletters. A more accurate assessment is that we had exhausted our resources in Atlanta and needed to till more fertile soil. Every rent check, every piece of clothing and every bite of food we used or consumed was provided for us through donations.

We stood at the front of churches across two continents, chastising Christians for not remembering the poor. We'd convert the lives of those whom we tended into "stories" to tell on Sunday morning, and the more we exposed our guests, the more the people emptied their pockets into the collection plates. If we offered something vague like "Julie is suffering from a heroin addiction and we are housing her. We ask that you join us in prayer that she might overcome the heroin," it might bring in a few hundred dollars. But if we added details, "Julie works as a street prostitute making just a few quid for every sexual encounter. She is missing a front tooth and has an infection on her right leg from a heroin dose that was cut with rat poison. She's been working the streets since she was 13," for this added glimpse of darkness, their money would flow as easily as their Sunday tears. Our Sunday morning sales job was reminiscent of the antebellum slave auctions. We both commodified a human, capitalizing on their strengths and weaknesses for our gain. In our world, the weaker and more broken translated into the higher prize. We would leave those Sunday solicitations with our bellies and our pockets full, and by the time we paid the bills, there was little left to effectively serve the poor. We incorporated them into our poverty, using their status of "indigent" to justify our own.

For seven long years we lived within the chaos and noise of poverty. One day after dropping my children off at school, I walked back home the long way and ended up at a duck pond. I started to sit down on a tiny section of green but discovered it was covered in duck poo. So, instead, I stood on the graveled bank in the middle of that busy city and watched the ducks swim from one end of the lake to the other. There was the mama duck swimming in that cold water with five little chicks in tandem behind her. I watched those ducks swim back and forth, tucking their beaks under the water for a little nibble now and then until time slowed, and then eventually stopped. I just stood there staring as if in a trance, hoping, wishing, begging those ducks to answer questions I didn't know how to ask. The wild confusion and thrashing noise of the city of my head became still, and in the quiet of those eternal moments, I knew I would leave my husband. I also knew that before I could, I would have to leave God. My marriage was intricately wound around Christian duty and expectations, and I would not be able to quit one without the other.

The mama duck began banging her wings against the water, and I guessed she was churning up the velocity required to fly. For a moment, she did take flight. But it was just to a stretch of water a few feet in front of her. When her wings were out and flapping, I saw that one of them was damaged, maybe a fish or another duck had taken a bite out of it. As I walked away to pick up my children at the school gate, I was encouraged by the mama duck. I did not have to make a winter migration and travel thousands of emotional miles to make my break. I could spread my own damaged wings and lurch forward just enough to find fresh opportunities under the surface of my life. I underestimated the effort of that small lurch. My execution, much like the mama duck, was inelegant and unsophisticated, but that small shift in the stagnant pond of my life changed everything. After my flapping frenzy of flight, I found a blessed silence.

We Have a Situation Here

WHEN I FIRST began writing to Antoinette, back when the idea of a book was more a shadow and less a concrete form, I assumed her relationship with her defense attorneys, the Brays, would prohibit her from responding to me. But I had underestimated Antoinette Davis. While I was busy vigorously and unsuccessfully attempting to pull information from her defense attorney, D.W. Bray, and other Fayetteville officials, Antoinette, with careful consideration and a good dose of fear, responded to one of my letters. Her handwriting was tidy, with printed words in large letters. She had handwritten it in blue ink on lined, prison-issued paper. It was a short letter expressing her fear of my intentions. She told me she did not trust the media and wanted my assurance that I would not exploit her or malign her daughter's name for my own gain.

Among the flutter of letters that landed in her jail cell from me, one asked a series of questions that I included as an icebreaker. They were leftover questions from my teaching days that were meant to disarm frightened students. But these questions, which I had listed in numbered form, bristled Davis.

In that first letter, she explained that she would not answer my questions because she felt it was an attempt to profile her for my book. I was struck by her caution and refusal. The questions sought such innocuous information as her favorite ice cream flavor (chocolate almond chip) or if she is tidy or messy (tidy). Her refusal helped me see my request from her point of view. I asked intimate details of her habits and lifestyle. In a bumbling attempt to quash her fears, I had treated her like a goat in a petting zoo. She felt invaded and paraded. I silently cursed myself as I read her letter, fearing that I had blown my chance to understand her. Trust is a fledging and requires constant, careful attention, and I felt that my clumsiness had been accidentally destructive.

But Antoinette, despite being nothing like me, was a lot like me. She was curious, and perhaps because she had spent most of her life in one long inhale of pain and betrayal, she seemed ready for her exhale. She was willing to try with me. Soon the letters began to flow between us, which led to long discussions of how we could connect by phone. Setting up these phone calls was a sluggish affair that required third-party billing and multiple letters mailed back and forth to pin down exact times that I could accept the calls. Time moves very slowly in prison. There is no sense of immediacy there. Time hangs, and within that suspension, old fashioned virtues of anticipation and wonder and patience emerge. Our first planned phone call took almost five weeks to coordinate.

About the same time I started my research for this book, my twin started up a boutique Internet bakery. She would mail the "extras" to her family and friends with a little note like, "just past the shelf date but knew they would still be delicious" or "tried out a new chocolate chip but wasn't satisfied." The lucky recipient would find a box full of gorgeous brownies on her front steps that, to the untrained eye, appeared flawless. We would shrug our shoulders and dig in. It seemed disgraceful to let a perfectly good brownie go to waste. And this arrangement worked quite well for me. I was her twin and by default, her all-time favorite relative. But then she created her pecan tart, and things went a bit wild after that. Firstly, it was delicious, sticky and crunchy on top of buttery, flaky pastry. Secondly, just about the time she perfected the pecan tart, she trained herself on the shrink-wrap machine. These two events collided to form an abundance, a manna from heaven abundance of pecan tarts arriving at my door. "Tried a darker brown sugar on these, what do you think?" the little elegant note would read. And, then, "I messed up the @#$! shrink-wrap again but the product is delicious." She adopted the Samuel Beckett motto of "try, fail, try again, fail better."

The trouble, as it became evidently clear with my straining shirt buttons and exhausted zippers, was that her pecan tart *was* delicious. So, it became my habit to come home from work, grab a brownie, and check my phone messages with unrealistic hope that Antoinette had called, then fire up an episode of *The Good Wife* before Simeon arrived home. On this particular day, a Tuesday, I did not vary from my routine. I struggled with the shrink-wrap on my pecan tart bar as I navigated the TV menu to find my show. Shrink-wrap is a tenacious invention that requires one to exhibit skills in patience, ingenuity and, in the inevitable end, direct assault. I was distracted by the sealed tart when I hit "play" on my answering machine. Suddenly the brownie and *The Good Wife's* Alicia Florrick, both of which captivated my interest day after day, became insignificant.

The machine, in its slow, mechanical voice, told me I had missed a call. Nothing too alarming there, landlines are predictable receptacles for the dying art of telemarketing. I expected a home security system or to hear the horn from a cruise ship offer but instead heard, "You have a collect call from [and then I heard her actual voice say] 'Antoinette Davis.' This is a call from the Raleigh Correctional Institution for Women. This call will be monitored and recorded. If you wish to accept this call press five." I dropped the half-clawed-open tart onto the carpet and stared at the phone as if it could answer all my soul-aching questions. Antoinette Davis called me? I played the message again; my hand was shaking as I hit *rewind* and then *play*. It had finally happened.

After all our planning and letter writing, she finally found the courage to call me. If she had known me, she would have laughed at the thought that she needed courage to call me. I was the coward. I taped the recording—which sounds a bit redundant, but I wanted a copy on my phone to keep as a talisman.

When I began feeling like I lost my way in this book, on this venture, and these feelings crept into my busy brain several times a day, I could play that recording, and it would serve as my compass. I didn't precisely know where I was going on this journey, or even, sometimes, why I was taking it. But this research, this book had become a vocation. Now Antoinette Davis had called and I felt a rush of hope and direction. I knew she didn't fully understand what I was trying to do; she couldn't possibly understand because even *I* didn't get it.

Either-which-way, she had called, and I danced with great joy around my living room. No more pecan tarts, damn it, it was time to start behaving like a proper writer. This meant, of course, that I must write. It would make good sense to say that I sat down with a renewed fervor and began to write. But this is precisely what I did not do. I called my husband, Simeon, to tell him the news. "Order the expensive pizza." He laughed. "We are going to celebrate."

And so began two weeks' worth of waiting for Antoinette to call me again. I wrote up a list of questions that I wanted to ask her, constantly tweaking and adding to it as I waited. Finally, she called back, and I was ready. Or, anyway, I naïvely *assumed* I was ready. I had my list by the phone with a recording device so I could replay the conversation in case I couldn't take notes fast enough. The message, which was now memorized in my head because I had played the recording back so many times, began, "You have a call from [pause and some clicking sounds] 'Antoinette Davis'" . . . and I waited with my finger poised above the "5." When the prison recording (finally) stopped I pressed "5" to accept. "Antoinette?" I called out, I was so nervous. "Is this Antoinette Davis?" I asked. In reply to my questions, I received another recording telling me to hit "7" to "set up an inmate account." I thought I had taken care of all that online already. I panicked because I could not let her know that I was on the other side of the line eagerly following the rules so we could finally speak. I worried she would take the silence as a rejection. I patiently and obediently followed all the instructions, pressing this number to proceed and that number to agree to the terms. Eventually, I was asked to put in my credit card number and then *that* was read back to me by the recording with the computer voice raising on every "two" so it sounds like a question: 472(?) 34884 82(?)9.

I was prompted to interact with this machine by pressing "1" for correct and "4" for incorrect, then we did the whole dance again for the expiration date and, by now my heartbeat had slowed down so significantly I feared I might be in a trance. Finally, finally, I was asked to enter and then confirm the secret code, which is no secret at all, found on the back of the card. There. Finished. I did it and I felt a similar sense of achievement as when I walked across the stage to receive my graduate degree or that Tom Cruise felt when going back up into the ceiling after hanging upside down to upload files from the nerve center of the CIA in *Mission Impossible*.

I was going to actually speak with Antoinette. After all this time, all this energy, through all my confusion and even in my moments of acute clarity, I was irrevocably going to speak with her. I heard some more clicking and the by now familiar machine voice said, "The calling party has hung up." I stared at the phone, cursing the machines that worked within it and because it made no sense to continue holding the receiver to my ear, I hung up.

Attempt failed. I shot off a note to Antoinette, telling her to please, please, for the love of God (later I would discover that I chose the wrong term because she had converted to the Islam faith shortly after entering prison), please call me back. I needn't have worried. Dollie Bray notwithstanding, Antoinette was on her own journey of discovery and was quite willing and excited to call me back. And so we began a weekly and then twice weekly phone visit to supplement our letters. These endeavors were expensive. Prisons have become a lucrative business now that many of them have become privatized, and phone calls cost twenty-two cents per minute. These calls are recorded and limited to fifteen minutes each. It is an automated system that announces the time ticking down with a pleasant female voice interjecting into our conversation, "You have sixty seconds remaining." It startled me every time and caused me to become a chatter-box—just chatting about nonsense allowing Antoinette no room to respond—up to the second warning of, "You have thirty seconds remaining," at which time I would double my speed and end up talking to dead air because the call had been disconnected. "Antoinette?" I questioned. "Are you there?" but she was gone. I recorded all of our conversations and they all end with me muttering "damn it," into the lonely space of a one-sided conversation.

But these phone calls and letters facilitated a strange and unnatural relationship. At first, I peppered her with prepared questions, and she would answer like she was taking an exam. But, later, as our guards lowered and we found our way together, the conversations became warm. For the first few months, we talked about everything except the crime. We talked about her hopes of becoming a Navy Seal and her love of the ROTC. I told her about my torn feelings between not liking marriage but madly loving my husband. Men were a big focus of those early months. She was determined to find a boyfriend and had joined some kind of prison matching service, but the men who wrote to her were of such low character. They all wanted something from her. "Send me a picture of yourself naked" type of guys, needy and organ driven.

But even as we eased into a comfortable rhythm of conversing and writing, we both maintained shields of protection. I didn't trust that she was telling me the truth about her knowledge of the crimes, and she didn't trust me that I wouldn't exploit her story and further damage her reputation. I offered to put $50 on her prison books once a month to cover her expenses in writing to me. I wanted to keep the integrity of our relationship solid, but at the same time, we were caught in a system of exchange.

My needs were more straightforward; I wanted her story. Her needs were much more hidden and confusing. She needed someone to believe her innocent (I sometimes did, sometimes didn't) and someone on the "outside" to care for her. There were moments in our exchanges when I felt a profound connection to her and she felt dear and essential to me. But other times I felt she saw me as her "sugar daddy" and imagined her laughing in her cell with her friend Adrianne at her "stupid white bitch" who sent her books and letters and money. There was no way to reconcile these conflicting viewpoints. Antoinette felt the same dichotomy concerning me. How could I offer one hand in true friendship without taking something from her with the other? As much as I despised Lockhart and his clean getaway from the disaster he helped to create, I likened myself to him when it came to Antoinette. I was only able to offer conditional "love." I held the authority in the relationship in that Antoinette's situation demanded that she be powerless. This made me the power holder. And I did openly want something from her that would result in my gain. Her story, as she often reminded me, was "big and important." I intended to sell this story for a profit. Antoinette could never receive any gain from her story, and while I promised her a portion of the proceeds to be held for her as my gift when she is released (seventeen years from now), how can she trust that? I barely trust that.

So we danced along in this alternate reality, one where I pretended I mattered to her and she pretended she could believe in me. Antoinette is a person who knows the literal implications of losing everything—children, family, home, autonomy and even the right to be called by a name. I have nothing to lose. Even if my book remains stashed in my bedroom closet, I still have my Simeon, my twin, my children; my life is a full and happy one. And still I am drawn to Antoinette. Her presence in my head and then later in my life has altered me. I have shifted ideas and beliefs around to make room for her. She no longer represents the guilty or bad parts of me. Her courage to choose to trust me, despite a lifetime of experiences that taught her to internalize vulnerability and protect herself at all costs, has softened me.

She has been attacked and exposed by the American public as monstrous and cruel. And yet, every day she gets up from her prison cot and somehow stands under judgment. She bears the weight of the collective hate that presses upon her and chooses to go to school and work her prison landscape job. I had cut off parts of me to survive. I excised my heart and allowed my brain to call the shots in my life. But she laughs with her friend Adrianne and talks to me as a full person, not one who has a vacancy carved out where her heart is meant to be housed. Antoinette represents hope, and I find myself wanting to imitate her in some small way.

Agitated and Pressed

W<small>HILE</small> I <small>WAITED</small> for Antoinette to respond to my letters, my research, inevitably and unfortunately, led me to her defense attorney, D.W. Bray and his formidable wife, Dollie. I had watched enough *Dateline* to know that defense attorneys love the camera, and while I may lack Keith Morrison's sexy allure, I certainly matched his enthusiasm. I expected the Brays to be relieved, perhaps even grateful that I had approached them for insight into this crime. But this was a grave miscalculation. They avoided my calls, emails and letters for the first five weeks. By then my husband and I had already mapped a geographic research trip to Fayetteville. This was two years after the sentencing.

The then Fayetteville Police Chief, Tom Bergamine, in addition to the Brays, was equally evasive. This evasion was surprising, considering the fact that his main job, the one the good people of Fayetteville hired him to do, was to talk to the public about the high profile cases. Through my long months of research, the Fayetteville Police Department Public Relations Officer never spoke with me despite my rigorous and sometimes obsessive efforts. The Brays, however, were a different animal altogether. Unlike a statement from the Public Liaison Officer, which would add to the story but would not be essential, I needed a statement from the Brays. They had authority over Antoinette and, at the time, were her gatekeepers.

The Brays remained strangely tight-lipped about the case during our phone calls; they didn't overtly shoo me away. That came later. My miscalculation gripped me in regret during the early stages of my research. I had spoken with Bray who assured me that Antoinette received hundreds of letters each day and that mine would end up in the trash unopened just like the others. Bray's wife, Dollie, added, "She won't talk to you without my say-so." She said it as a threat and it was one I took seriously.

Dollie had become very close to Antoinette during the four years between Shaniya's death and Antoinette's sentencing. Mrs. Bray had taken on a protective role, which is an understated way to express her stance regarding Antoinette. She was less a mama bear and more a determined, snarling wolf. And Dollie was clearly the alpha dog of her husband's practice.

She scared me. Bray told me that day that she would not allow me access to Antoinette. She was opposed, indeed offended by my approach to the book.

When I finally met the Brays, I dropped in on them without a formal appointment. I called ahead and spoke with their very nervous secretary, Melissa. I also sent an email letting D.W. know that I was coming to town and would like to stop by to plead my case in person. I received no response from her but moved forward as if I had been invited.

When I arrived at her office, I was overtaken by the smell. It immediately brought me back to the best of our childhood, sitting in the back of my grandpa's huge, ivory Chevrolet with my sister on our way to an overnight with our grandparents. Grandpa Powell was a chain smoker, and in the 1970s he would have received no admonishing looks from fellow travelers as he drove down the highway, windows all closed up tight and the car filled with the haze of that white, swirling smoke. My grandparents' house had that same distinct odor of old ashes and stale smoke. As soon as I opened the Bray's office door I was launched into the backseat of that cream colored Chevrolet. I took this as a good harbinger. But like everything I said or did in that office, I would be wrong.

Neither of the Brays was in the office when I arrived; I was instead greeted by their secretary who knew me from my frequent phone calls. Melissa was wearing a New England Patriot's sweatshirt and had a cigarette sitting in one of those old fashioned ashtrays that had a glass-type bowl attached to a little sandbag. The ashtray was full of butts with some sections so full they sat double-decker on top of each other. The cigarette had been sitting there for some time because it had burned into ash almost to the filter, producing a phantom of the shape it once was. There was a prescription bottle sitting next to the sandbag. I introduced myself with a false confidence, and put out my hand to her. She reached to shake my hand. The movement bumped the desk enough to shake that long ash away from the cigarette. She didn't seem to notice. I sat down without being asked when Melissa began to explain that the Brays would be unable to see me. Apparently, I had upset Dollie in one of my numerous emails. Melissa spoke quietly, but with authority. "You mentioned that you were going to offer McNeill the same treatment as Antoinette, and Dollie won't stand for it." She didn't know I was never interested in writing about McNeill and was only trying to assuage them. She kept glancing above my head to the entrance, and I began to sweat, worried that I was trespassing and that if Bray showed up, I would be bounced out to the smoke-free zone on the sidewalk. I tried to assure Melissa that I meant no offense and repeated for what felt like the millionth time, that I was not a media hound trying to capitalize on Davis' story. But she was hearing none of it. She had been tasked, I speculated, to get me out of the office before the Brays returned from their lunch. She had underestimated my resolve.

Had I known what was in store, I would have run for the door as the prairie dog runs from the wolf. I was only there a few minutes when Melissa's demeanor changed, and I felt, rather than observed, Dollie Bray and her entourage enter the building. Melissa immediately stood up, a look of terror frozen across her face. She moved to the end of the desk and waited for instructions. Dollie walked toward her, a cigarette dangling between two long fingers that ended with even longer fingernails. Dollie took the seat of the secretary, telling her, "Shut your mouth and get out of here." Melissa happily complied as she grabbed her purse and left. I did not see her again for the seventy minutes that I remained in this office.

I was now face to face with Dollie Bray. Her eyes actually resembled a wolf's with their blue so icy that they could and did make my teeth chatter. I understood this fear from a time when I was in a position to cause it. When we were little girls, many people responded to our twinship with commentary and requests. "Wait, stand next to each other and smile," they might command. And we, dutiful and people-pleasing, would comply. "Okay," they would instruct. "Now frown," and we would frown our identical frowns while we were assessed. "The one on the right has more blemishes than the one on the left." And so it would go, my sister and I performing to an unsolicited panel of judges.

One day a classmate of ours, one neither of us knew very well, saw us together, and she was truly shaken. "There are two of you?" she shrieked. Several of the other students heard the fear in her voice and took notice.

"Yes," one of us replied, "we are twins." We waited for the expected response of "that's so cool," or "do you guys get each other mixed up?" or some other twin remark.

But this girl was genuinely scared. "Don't look at me, you're witches. DON'T LOOK AT ME." She fled the cafeteria with my sister and me standing among our peers, feeling mortified but, in some small way, empowered.

Dollie Bray scared people, but she had done it for so long that she had found a way to harness power from their fear. She told me to pack up and get out. She had not yet looked at me, nor had she introduced herself. "I'm going to tell you right now that you'll not get a word out of me," she added in a voice so loud I felt certain my husband could hear it all the way from the car. "Put that away," she commanded, pointing at my recording device.

I scrambled to get it into my bag as she took the first of what would be hundreds of drags on her cigarette. She inhaled with gusto, sucking in with such angry authority that I watched with anticipation that her lips would crush the filter.

In one of the earlier email exchanges with her, I made the mistake of mentioning McNeill's name next to Antoinette's. It was this geographic positioning, her client's name next to a killer, that bristled Bray. She despised McNeill with such dedication that her conversation fell tilted to one side. Her discussion about him sounded rehearsed, and I knew I was not the first to hear "despicable deadbeat" and "contemptible convict" uttered from her quick, loud mouth. In the seventy minutes we spent together, she asked me to leave her office three separate times. At her first request, I began to gather my things, but she kept talking through my packing up, and so I remained seated and very quiet and she seemed to forget that she had kicked me out. I called upon this strategy twice more throughout the interview.

As long as I was content to play the role of her audience, she was content to let me stay. But she made it clear that she did not like me and further, did not trust me. This last point was the kill shot to any hope I had for her assistance. She saw the media as a swarm of hornets, and she had the wounds to substantiate her claim. All of my protestations that I was not with a magazine or secretly recording her for the five o'clock news fell muted between us. Her words ran around, over and through all other dialogue in that room. I've studied linguistic techniques in graduate school but found no scholastic category for Bray's linguistic style. Her speech could not be dissected from her demeanor. She was angry, hostile, energetic and memorably passionate all at the same time. She held a certain physical beauty, which she played to her advantage. Not so much with me; I was beneath her notice. But by the way she moved and pushed back her hair, I could tell she understood her physical capital and used it as another weapon in her well-fortified arsenal.

Bray's boisterous objections to me could hardly be taken personally. Indeed, she didn't perform anything special for me; she approached all areas of her life with equal amounts of energetic intensity. I watched her speak about Antoinette with such aggression that I found myself physically recoiling from her adamant and loud proclamations. Her hatred toward McNeill was jarring as she shouted during discovery that McNeill's phone held multiple sexual images of children. Bray recognized one of the children as a child of her family friend. It was this photo that fueled her rage. Yes, she represented Antoinette whose little girl had been violated by McNeill, but she also knew and loved a child who had survived McNeill's violation. Her disgust for him was personal.

She is a tiny woman in all ways but volume. She was a dog whistle, a small, simple-looking device that can produce frequencies unmanageable to the human ear. It wasn't just Bray's volume that kept me on high alert during our interview. When she snapped her cigarette pack against the palm of her hand, I initially took the action as a threat. *Smack, smack,* she hit her hand with that pack, and I watched, quietly, as she pulled at a cigarette and in one involuntary motion, had it extricated from the box and into her mouth and lit. I didn't even see her light it. It was like watching the parasympathetic nervous system work to produce a blink. Everything is happening behind the scenes but for the result.

It was to my advantage in that meeting that Dollie Bray smoked almost continuously. Her brain was so intense and so fast that I needed her long and desperate inhale on that cigarette to gain some time for my own brain synapses to catch up. She was less a hammer beating at a nail and more a nail gun set to an automatic trigger. Even the most skillful brain may dodge one or two missiles, but her speed and accuracy would eventually overtake her audience, and like all those gathered around her, I mostly sat in a smoky muted state of awe. Bray isn't the queen of her kingdom; she is its goddess.

When I finally was ejected from that smoky, excited room, I approached the car in a kind of heady stupor. I had been "Brayed." When we were quite young, our mom kept an old-fashioned, hand-cranked washing machine in the basement next to the electric one. It was a complicated machine that required us to turn the handle, pressing two rods that looked like fat rolling pins against each. The rollers pressed the water out of the clothes so when they squeezed through to the other side, they were stiff and flat from the process. They could stand on their own from the pressing. When I left the Bray's office, I felt like a pair of jeans that had been squashed through that old washing machine. I could stand but felt that the life juice had been pressed from me.

Bray had reminded me that Antoinette would not write to me without her consent and I could hardly blame Antoinette, a shy, soft-spoken uneducated woman, for acquiescing to Bray's insistence that she not respond to me. After I met Bray for myself, I sometimes felt guilty when writing to Antoinette. My heart rate increased, and I worried that Bray would find out and somehow stop me, or worse, confront me. Bray had offered herself as refuge to Davis back when the situation happened. That's what Antoinette calls it: "my situation." Davis, who was being pursued by an army of media shouting groupthink slogans of "abominable" and "evil," may have believed that she had a chance standing behind Bray. But even Bray, with all her Erin Brockovich bravado, could not shelter Antoinette from the ensuing and seemingly eternal storm that raged and beat against her. Bray may have been able only to offer an umbrella in the middle of a hurricane, but it was the offering itself that bound the two women together.

Mirror, Mirror

Antoinette's journey to the North Carolina Correctional Institute was arguably longer and more painful than mine, which is why I often reproached myself when complaining about how difficult it was to finally visit her there. Antoinette's presence in this crime has always been problematic for me. I wanted to write a story about a bad man who did a bad thing and who now wears the orange jumpsuit. When I finally narrowed down my *Murderpedia* search and chose Mario McNeill, I realized that Antoinette Davis was inexplicably bound to him. I could not write about him without including her. Nor, I realized as I slogged deeper into this story, could I write about her without writing about me.

Initially, I saw Antoinette much as I had always seen McNeill, a bad person who had done a bad thing. I assumed I could visit her in her "jail world" to learn all I needed to know from her perspective of this story. In graduate school, I learned the difference between primary and secondary sources and was many times called upon to use the secondary source to help define the primary. For example, I might be asked to examine Plato's *Allegory of the Cave* by discussing an episode from the television series *Lost*. Initially, I suspected the information I gained from Antoinette would join a long list of secondary sources that would help me understand and analyze the primary source. The primary source, in the early stages of my research brain, was the rape and murder of Shaniya Davis. But as I slowly trudged through the marshlands of the human condition, I found myself sinking into the muck of something familiar. While I never lived in a trailer park or made purchases from drug dealers, I fully understood deprivation. I wanted a tidy distance between my side of the jailyard fence and Antoinette's. The bad people lined up in Antoinette's story on an opposite side of the good people in my life like a childhood game of Red Rover. Only the closer I ran to her side of the line, the more I recognized myself.

When I was in my young twenties, I accepted a job as a summer camp counselor at a girl's camp up in Maine. I had never been that far apart from my twin sister, and I was scared as I packed up my little clunker car in preparation for my three-state sojourn from Ohio to Maine. "Kerri, please, please come up and visit me this summer," I begged my sister.

"You never know, Abigail, I might just show up one night during campfire."

I pulled away and drove almost fourteen hours to get to the camp. I arrived too early in the morning for any administrators to check me in, so I took myself on a tour of the camp. This was before the Internet, so I had no sneak-peek photo album to acquaint myself with my new summer home. I wandered through the woodsy huts and tents and eventually ended up at an impressive log-cabin-type structure with a folksy wooden sign announcing it as "The Camp Theater."

This was the building I would work in alongside two writer/directors who were rumored to have been a big splash on Off Broadway in New York. I would be their apprentice counselor. I wandered through this beautiful building that was lit by long floor-to-ceiling windows showing off the Maine forest and nearby lake. I walked up on the stage and took a bow to an imaginary crowd but couldn't wait to get backstage as I knew that is where I would spend most of my hours helping the girls for their performances. I nosed around a bit when I heard something from the other side of the stage. Standing there in front of the windows was my sister. I couldn't believe it! It was just like her to plan an elaborate surprise. She had secretly followed me all the way up to Maine and now here she was at the summer camp. I started running toward her at full speed, overjoyed that I wouldn't have to spend the summer without her. I threw my arms open as I prepared to plow into her hug when *smack*! I hit my nose on something so hard it knocked me down. I was shocked and deeply confused until I realized that I was sitting in front of a full length mirror. I had run into myself.

That unexpected impact is what it felt like as I ran full force into Antoinette's story. I needed her to be different from me; I needed her to be the bad one so I could be the good one. I felt certain I recognized the landscape of her life and her story as separate from mine, but as I pushed toward it, I ran into myself. Antoinette, regardless of her innocence or guilt in the criminal court system, is not any more innocent or guilty than I am. There was, of course, a fortified distance between our sides of the fence, but that distance had little to do with guilt.

Flashlight

When I first approached Antoinette, she was careful and shy. I sent her a generic letter, formal and typed, asking for her insights into Shaniya's rape and murder. Like McNeill, who received a similar letter, she did not respond. I wrote again, this time a handwritten card assuring her that I wanted to examine every lens in this textured kaleidoscope. I tried to explain my intent of analyzing the crime through the idea of our commonality. I faithfully raced to my mailbox every day and still no letter. I kept at it, writing to her once a week and all the while digging through the volumes of written text surrounding the case. I created elaborate charts and time-lines. I made a family tree for Antoinette and discovered a deficient root system incapable of supporting so much fruit. Her great-grandmother, Hunter Blue, bore eight children, many of whom successfully matched that number with their own offspring. The women in her family bore the fruit with the men never joining the tree but growing up near it, like weeds blown in from another place. Antoinette was just 25 years old when she went to prison, but she too was already following her family's tradition of multiple fathers for multiple children, children who became her sole responsibility.

Simeon and I made a weekend get-away out of a Fayetteville research trip, hoping to ripple the pond with a few pebbles of interest. I did not expect to find such fortified fencing around this story. No one wanted to talk with me concerning this case. I made a list of twenty-eight key locations to visit and even with several emails and phone calls to the people connected with these locations beforehand, the townsfolk maintained a strict stiff-arm policy. I logged dozens of phone calls to the Fayetteville Police Department, each one ending with my frustration at their closed loop attitude. Even the local people, those who had no professional affiliation with this crime or those convicted of it, were resistant to speak to me. One lady who worked at a Quick Stop was friendly and chatty until I asked her if she knew a more specific location of the first burial site of Shaniya. She looked away sharply as if I had slapped her. "Honey, I can't help you with that," she said and then abruptly walked away, leaving me to return my little can of Pringles to the shelf as it was clear she was not going to ring me up.

Additionally, I had contacted an acquaintance who was a close family friend of Judge Ammons. Ammons sat for both McNeill's trial and Davis' plea arrangement. I enthusiastically asked my friend for an informal letter of introduction. My attempts to contact Ammon's office had been unsuccessful. My friend responded in a similar fashion to the Quick Stop clerk. "We don't want to be involved," he told me over the phone. "You don't understand how much this crime affected Fayetteville."

I was surprised by his response and countered, "I think I do understand in that I am writing a book about that very issue, the fallout and repercussions of that night in November." I assured him that this book's intent was to facilitate a discussion that might lead to healing for his hometown. But he maintained his resolute stance, and I maintained my bewilderment at such a collective reluctance. Why were people so afraid to discuss this case? I doubted that it was due to the depravity of the crime, but more due to a personal discomfort in examining the case within the prickly and potentially horrifying truth that very little separated the sheep from the goats.

Many years ago I attempted to hold Glen legally responsible for his crimes against my sister and me. A statute of limitations was in effect, so I could not pursue criminal charges against him. There was, however, one small caveat in the Ohio State Law that I intended to invoke. If I could present sufficient evidence to an educated panel, then I had a shot at placing Glen on the Sexual Predator List. I secured an attorney who filed all the motions, which resulted in a formal interview with John Ferrero, District Attorney of Stark County.

I recounted my experience in a small conference room that contained pictures of the then governor and two members of the D.A.'s team. Their task was to determine if there was enough evidence to move forward with the motion. It was a harrowing interview that involved, among other things, standing in front of one of the assistant D.A.s (the only female on the team) and, pretending she was Glen, point to any geographic body locations that held distinguishing marks that would not be visible in a swimsuit. Despite their thoroughness, my case was seen as flimsy. I would be facing a "he said/she said" paradigm. It would be my word against his and his word came with some social capital. Glen was a well-respected, faithful, church-going man. In this case, the process, as it was intended to do, would protect the "accused-until-proven-guilty" creed we all depend upon when facing a charge or allegation. The only recourse I would have to break this stalemate would be to provide forensic or eyewitness testimony that would refute his protestations.

So I was forced to turn to my twin. It's an ironic consideration that I was lucky to have a twin who could testify to the veracity of my claim. Adult survivors of sexual abuse have very little hope at achieving justice without acknowledging another person who knew of or was victim to the abuse. Not all casualties of such a childhood have the courage or even the interest to pursue such legal options, however limiting they may be. My twin was among their numbers.

She handled the suffering of our childhood in a completely different way than I did. "You want to heal out loud," she once told me. "I prefer to heal in quiet." My request that she substantiate my claim became a heated and dividing line in our twinship. At first, she avoided the topic, hoping her reluctance would make it all go away. But I was not easily deterred and continued to press. Eventually, she began responding to my dialog but chose to include our genius brother into the conversation. I suspected she did this as a security measure. While my twin and I both were estranged from the family—our family reunion invitations had been revoked decades ago—my twin still sought to keep some connection to our lost family. Her attempts at connection were suggestions of a relationship, the shadow of the real thing. She left occasional comments on their Facebook pages, for example, or stopped by every few years for a cup of coffee when she was back in town. She extended these nuanced whispers to the peripheral family members. I never asked nor did she offer if she had attempted to assuage Glen in such manners. I would consider such attempt, no matter how trite, a betrayal.

My own family estrangement was based on the principal of my right to invoke an open discussion regarding our childhood. Like my twin, my brother and company preferred the *if we don't talk about it maybe it didn't really happen* technique popular in situations like this one. The standard operating procedure surrounding child abuse in general but sexual abuse in particular is to silence the victim through villainization. My family was no different, and in fact, their textbook response was to isolate and then silence. I trained my flashlight into the dark closet of their crimes of complicity and they, unable to discredit the light itself, concentrated on a thorough discrediting of the flashlight's owner. They preferred the darkness of deceit to the light of truth. In order to enhance their own protestations, they worked to diminish mine. It was then that my invitations to the family get-togethers were revoked. I was ostracized from family friends and discussed as "the crazy twin" or other such stigmatizing judgments. It was easier for my family to circle the predator and silence the prey than to allow any hint at impropriety that lay submerged in their genetic pool.

Eventually, my sister responded to my written indictment with a tarnish of her own. She believed my document to be "exaggerated" and "heavily influenced by my legal counsel." While she did not deny the abuse to the district attorney during her own phone interview, she would not testify to the details of my allegations. And so the legal maneuver was outmaneuvered and remains impotently filed within the D.A.'s office. The rat in question was never required to emerge from his dark hole, nor was there any legal recourse bright enough to expose him from where he hid. Humans have a great investment in maintaining status quo, even if the status is reprehensible.

The players in the Fayetteville case vacillated between gentle redirection and open rebukes when I showed up with my research flashlight. I could not account for their concerned dismissal of this case outside of the status quo theory. Their bad guys were in jail, and the rest of them were better by the comparison. But what about Brad Lockhart? He was not considered a villain in his hometown any more than Glen was in mine. Lockhart and Glen represent a certain ilk of men who prowl about their universe with an indemnity against any type of judgment written into their privileged DNA.

One third of American women, according to national statistics, have a predator swimming around in their aquariums. The statistics in my childhood represented a more forbidding narrative. One hundred percent of the female children in Glen's household navigated a predator in their hallway and bedroom and bath-room. Like Lockhart, Glen was able to shield himself through his church association and his esteemed standing in his family and community. Like Lockhart, Glen's advocates elevated his innocence by depreciating his victims' ethos.

My hypothesis scared my family as much as it scared the Fayetteville community. Bad people are not outside our sacred circles, but are rather within them. How could we continue with our status quo belief that we are somehow superior because of all those bad people who make inferior decisions? We hold to a faulty belief that *evil* is synonymous with *other* when the truth is that *evil* is synonymous with *human*. It is a necessary component of being alive. How can we claim the human condition as sacred if we cannot acknowledge our sins? Poverty and race and geographic situation do not hold claim to despicable behavior. It is found inside our own neighborhoods, our own families and our own hearts.

Collective Consequences

Brenda Davis

THROUGHOUT ALL OF the research for this book, Brenda Davis' role in the death of her niece remains unclear. Like her sister, Antoinette, there is no evidence to justify either her exoneration or her guilt in the crimes. Mario Andretti McNeill initially pled *not guilty* to his charges, but his proclamation was nuanced. While he staunchly denied any involvement in Shaniya's rape or death, he did admit to taking her from her home that night. He consistently maintained that he took her at the express request of his friend, the child's aunt, Brenda Davis. Strangely, the investigators made very little of McNeill's connection to Brenda. The two shared multiple text messages between them that night. The accounts differ here from forty to over sixty. Antoinette, on the other hand, sent and received zero text messages from McNeill, and not just on that night. Antoinette's and McNeill's phone records showed no contact between them, ever. Under interrogation, McNeill repeatedly stated that he did not know Antoinette other than as the sister of his sometimes lover, Brenda. A few facts seem to point to Brenda's association with the crimes. One, according to Brenda's own statements, she was the one who invited McNeill over that night. Two, she had recently moved into the Sleepy Hollow trailer, putting her name on the lease. According to Antoinette's defense team, Brenda's deposit owed for the trailer was $200.00. This is the same amount for which Antoinette allegedly sold Shaniya to McNeill, a rumor originating from a false statement in the coroner's report. The statement was later retracted by Billy West, Antoinette's prosecuting attorney. Three, Antoinette's toxicology report came back clean the next day. She had not been using drugs recent to the time of the incident. However, according to Antoinette, Brenda was actively involved in the drug culture at the time.

Had the investigation twisted itself in a slightly different manner, many published articles have argued that Brenda would be in prison, and Antoinette would have testified against her at trial instead of the other way around. But, from the beginning, the investigators had their eye on Antoinette, and I find their focused lens on her blurs their vision of Brenda. The high number of texts between Brenda and McNeill wasn't especially significant for him. He was a prolific texter and, according to FBI testimony, attempted to "hook up with twenty-six different women" before he made his way up Shaniya Davis' front steps.

All parties, including McNeill and the authorities, agree that it was Brenda who invited McNeill in that night. She and her boyfriend, JeRoy, wanted to "party" and she invited McNeill to bring the drugs. Brenda had a complicated relationship with McNeill, admitting on the stand that she slept with him on numerous occasions. She referred to their sexual relationship as "something to do." JeRoy's complicity with Brenda's wishes that evening adds a deeper level of confusion to an already bewildering night. He lived in the trailer with Brenda, who was not only considered his girlfriend, but the mother of his two children who also lived in the trailer. It's difficult to speculate why JeRoy might offer his endorsement for his girlfriend to invite over her casual sex partner. But the couple were avid drug users and perhaps this need squashed any apprehension he had concerning Brenda's propensity to have sex with their drug dealer. JeRoy was never indicted on any charges, and after the trials, he continued in his on-again-off-again relationship with Brenda. By October 2013, at McNeill's trial, Brenda would take the stand against McNeill while pregnant with JeRoy's third baby.

But on this night, Brenda and McNeill maintained a robust text communication throughout the evening until McNeill came into their trailer around three o'clock in the morning. Brenda, JeRoy and McNeill all admit to partying for several hours, according to McNeill's account, before Brenda asked him to take Shaniya from the home to find her a better living situation. McNeill told police interrogators that Brenda wanted Shaniya to live in a home where she could go to school. McNeill's prosecution attempted to persuade Brenda to indict Antoinette while under oath. She may have been offered immunity during initial questioning because she did testify against McNeill in his twelve-day trial. But her testimony lacked any true import in that she mainly spoke about facts already established and agreed upon by McNeill and the FBI. They wanted her to tell the court that Antoinette knew where her daughter was the morning she called 911 to report her missing. This would support their theory that Antoinette conspired with

McNeill to take Shaniya. But Brenda (BD) was not a convincing witness. When asked by the prosecutor, Billy West (BW), how Antoinette behaved when she "discovered" that her daughter was missing, she testified that her sister came into her bedroom:

> BD: *She asks us had we seen Shaniya.*
> BW: *Can you describe her demeanor at that point? How she was acting?*
> BD: *Um, she wasn't acting no kind of way.*
> BW: *And was Shaniya in your bedroom?*
> BD: *No.* [shaking head]
> BW: *What did you tell her?*
> BD: *Um, "No, she's not in here, she should be with you."*

Billy West goes on to ask her about what Antoinette's son, Carlesio, told her about a visitor to their home that night:

> BD: *He said, "Mono was here last night."*
> BW: *And Mono, he only knows one Mono?*
> BD: *Yes.*
> BW: *And who was that?*
> BD: *Mario.*
> BW: *The defendant?*
> BD: [Shakes head affirmatively]

Carlesio agreed with Brenda's testimony when it was his turn under oath. He told the court that the man inside their home that night had "dreadlocks, a goatee, gold teeth and was skinny-like," a description unmistakably matching McNeill. Neither Carlesio nor Brenda were asked by the prosecution if they knew who invited him in.

Brenda continued her testimony by discussing Antoinette's reaction when she saw McNeill for the first time after the abduction. Brenda testified that shortly after Shaniya "went missing" McNeill drove up to the trailer in a four-door, black car, asking to see Antoinette. Brenda told the court that Antoinette came out of the trailer enraged. Billy West questioned Brenda about what Antoinette said when she saw him:

BW: *What were her words that she screamed at the defendant?*
BD: *I don't give a* [redacted]. *I just wanna know where my* [redacted] *baby is.*

Brenda's role in or knowledge of the crime may never be known. The prosecution and the public were satisfied with the conviction of Antoinette and McNeill. Antoinette herself is circumspect when she considers her sister's role, saying that on the morning of November 10, Brenda acted strangely. Antoinette, in a phone call with me, relates that she remembers feeling frantic and frightened. She looked through the trailer ("It's only so big, Abigail") with Brenda standing in the living room staring at her. "She didn't help or ask any questions, she just stood there watching me." Whether or not Brenda knows all the details of how McNeill came to carry Shaniya out of that small trailer with a drug-addled aunt and a struggling mother inside, it remains clear that she knows more than she has told. With her older sister in jail for twenty years for crimes either one of them had means and opportunity to commit, she has little incentive to say anything at all.

Mario McNeill

Turning Himself In

Once the image of McNeill holding Shaniya in the Comfort Inn elevator bay was broadcast nationally,

McNeill turned himself in by calling the Fayetteville Police Department. Detective Elizabeth Culver was the responding officer at April Autrey's house on Washington Avenue. She testified that "he came willingly." Just before leaving his girlfriend, his children and his house for the last time in his life, he told Autrey, "You know what this is about." Autrey packed up the children and her belongings shortly after McNeill was arrested. She left behind everything that belonged to him, including his two dogs. The prosecution fussed over the state of the house as seen through the crime scene photos presented at trial. In particular, they wanted photos of the kitchen floor, which was covered in feces because the dogs had been left for several days after Autrey's departure. The defense attorney, Terry Alford, argued successfully that the pictures were prejudicial against McNeill. He argued unsuccessfully against the admission of pictures of a music CD called *Road Rash Jailbreak* with the lyrics:

> *rolling down the highway doing ninety*
> *going my way in control*
> *gotta watch those corners in the stretch of danger*
> *a problem could arise eventually* (Mad Caddies).

A problem did arise eventually. The judge allowed the CD photo into evidence as well as photos of motivational posters hung throughout the home. By the end of the twelve-day trial, the prosecution presented 44 witnesses and 451 evidentiary exhibits. The defense offered no witnesses and just one piece of evidence: Detective Culver's report of McNeill's arrest. Alford argued that by turning himself in, he "didn't walk in with a mask on; he just simply walked in." The defense felt that this action proved his innocence. *Why would a guilty man come to the station without protest?* McNeill refused to take the stand during his trial, asking only that the six-hour interrogation tape be played for the jury. He felt this would be enough to exonerate him of the charges. "The Culver Report," as it is called in the court transcripts, became McNeill's sole defense exhibit. To McNeill, it came down to how his willingness to get in Culver's car spoke to his innocence of the chargers. But, like Shaniya, he entered the car unaware that it would eventually lead him to his death.

Police Interrogation

McNeill did not do well in his police interviews. According to the documents, he was at times belligerent, exasperating, sleepy and disinterested. He started out typically enough; he denied everything. He claimed he didn't know Shaniya and that he had never seen her. When police showed him the now infamous picture of him cradling Shaniya in his arms as captured by the surveillance videos at the Sanford Comfort Inn, he replied, "That's not me." Eventually, McNeill changed his story to say that he knew Shaniya and furthermore had taken her, with permission from her aunt. The FBI watched the first few hours of McNeill's interview and advised the Fayetteville Police Department to keep McNeill talking. At this point, Shaniya had not been found and there was still hope she was alive. But McNeill was difficult to keep engaged. At one point he fell asleep during interrogations and had to be awakened and moved around the room to keep him awake. McNeill admitted to being "skied up" on cocaine. McNeill's use of cocaine came up in his trial.

Comfort Inn front desk clerk Regina Bacani testified that a housekeeper came to her with a small packet of white residue she found in room 201 after McNeill had checked out. Bacani told the court that she thought it was cocaine. She claimed that her manager threw it in the trash. This testimony supported McNeill's claim that he used cocaine that morning in the hotel with Shaniya in his custody. But he was less forthcoming about other activities that occurred in the room.

During the six hours of interviewing, McNeill sometimes closed his eyes and giggled. When he did choose to participate in the questioning, McNeill told police that he received a text from Brenda Davis to remove Shaniya and take her to the hotel to wait for a relative to pick her up. According to the FBI agent's testimony during McNeill's trial, McNeill admitted that he "had her in the motel and that he had cocaine." Fayetteville Police Sergeant Chris Corcione (CC) was the lead questioner in McNeill's interviews. Corcione told McNeill, "You have more information than I do."

McNeill replied, "Actually, I haven't."

Corcione, driven by the hope of finding Shaniya alive, pressed McNeill:

> CC: *You like to [molest] little girls. That's what everybody is thinking.*
>
> MM: *A long time ago I stopped worrying about what everybody thinks.*
>
> CC: *I need you to do the right thing and tell me where this princess is. What are you hiding, buddy?*
>
> MM: *I have nothing to hide.*

Later in the questioning, McNeill revealed he "didn't think it would go this far." When Corcione pressed him to disclose where Shaniya was, McNeill repeated, "I don't know. I don't know. I don't know."

> CC: *You killed that baby, didn't you?*
>
> MM: *No, no, no.*
>
> CC: *We can't accept that. We have a missing 5-year-old girl who was in your possession.*
>
> MM: *Do you have your evidence? You have everything you have. Do what you have to do.*
>
> FBI Agent: *You admit having her between Fayetteville and Sanford.*
>
> MM: *I take everything I said back. I make bad decisions sometimes.*

When McNeill was left alone in the interrogation room, he used his cell phone saying, "They're trying to charge me with everything. Everybody's calling me and texting me about it now."

But things would get worse for McNeill. The FBI agent testified that during his questioning, McNeill shocked his questioners when he stated that he was "waiting to get a call to come and kill her." Cumberland County Assistant District Attorney Robby Hicks (RH) battered McNeill while questioning the FBI agent on the stand:

> RH: *Did he [McNeill] use a word that changed the focus of the testimony?*
>
> FBI: *At one point he said he was "waiting to get a call to come and kill her."*
>
> RH: *How did you respond?*
>
> FBI: *The interviewers, everybody, kind of stopped. I asked McNeill, "What did you say?" He actually said he was "waiting to come and kill her."*

The FBI agent told the court that he attempted to convince McNeill to explore that statement but he was unsuccessful.

McNeill's defense attorney, Terry Alford (TA), was unable to diminish the damage of this testimony:

TA: *Did Mario correct himself later in that interview?*

FBI: *He corrected himself to say that he was waiting for someone to "get her," not "kill her."*

But this retraction became a minor footnote during his trial. Even with scant forensic evidence—his DNA was never found on her body—the video of him holding Shaniya in the hotel lobby caused more damage than his defense team could repair.

Problems in Court

Two notable problems occurred during McNeill's trial and both had to do with poor behavior. Courtrooms are formal places with severe rules and armed guards standing by to enforce these rules. As much as television shows make entertainment about what happens in court, the inside of a courtroom is considered sacrosanct in that one or more parties has entered the space with a loss large enough to require a judge to weigh the consequences of that loss. People are meant to be on their best behavior in court. The person sitting at the defense table is expected to act with the highest amount of courtesy to the court and the justice system because he has the most to lose. But McNeill did not choose to play his role this way. When the FBI Agent left the stand, he had to walk by McNeill who called him a liar. Prosecuting Attorney Hicks held a sidebar with Judge Ammons (JA) during the jury's lunch break:

RH: *I ask that the defendant not say these things to my witness.*

MM: *I asked why he was lying.*

Later in the trial, the prosecution presented photographs taken by the coroner of Shaniya's body.

Ammons noticed that several people sitting behind *the* defense table were behaving poorly.

> JA: *I saw several people laughing and making inappropriate comments and gestures about the child's body.*

He addressed his comments to Juanita Ball (JB), McNeill's mother:

> JB: *These people are not with me.*
> JA: *I'm not going to tolerate this.*

The second issue of behavior rested on McNeill's demeanor in the courtroom. He spent much of the trial sitting at a messy defense table, using random papers to meticulously fold origami shapes. His actions were taken as a mockery of the court proceedings. At one point Judge Ammons yelled at him to stop folding origami. McNeill had just refused his mother a chance to speak on his behalf. She had walked up to the witness box and had been sworn in but McNeill did not want her to speak. Judge Ammons (JA) held her in the box while he questioned McNeill on his decision. It's possible Ammons was attempting to dismiss any appeal that might arise from McNeill not allowing his lawyers to put on a defense. Ammons asked McNeill to tell his mother that he didn't want her to testify. Juanita Ball sat in the box with her back straight, not touching the back of her chair. She was in a teal dress with a matching jacket. Her teal pearls hung in two tidy rows beneath her drawn face. She sat muted by her son, waiting for his permission to speak:

> JA: *Will you tell your mother you do not want her testify on your behalf?*
> MM: [looking at his mother] *I do not want you to testify on my behalf. Love you.*

JA: *Do you want her to testify? Will you give her a chance to put this evidence on?*
[eight-second silence in courtroom]
MM: *No.*

The judge was upset by McNeill's decisions as they both watched the frail but proud-looking woman dismantle herself from the box and walk back to her seat in the gallery behind McNeill's defense table. She carried a white handkerchief, which she used to dab her eyes as she walked to her seat. This distressed Ammons:

JA: *Do you clearly understand that you can be put to death?* [starts to put glasses on]
MM: *Yeah.*
JA: [takes glasses back off] *Is that your desire?*
MM: *No.*
JA: *Then tell me why you won't let your lawyers try to help you.*
MM: *I wanted my freedom. I lost my freedom; what else matters out there?*
[Defense Attorney] TA: *McNeill has instructed me not to participate in the sentencing, hearing or offer any closing. Obviously, that's against our wishes, against our desire, against our professional opinion. We are at an impasse.*
JA: [responding to McNeill's seeming smile] *Is there anything that would change your mind? It bothers me that you think this is funny, but maybe this is a coping mechanism. They can take you to Raleigh and execute you, do you understand that?*
MM: *Yeah.*
JA: *I don't mean any disrespect, but this is a little more important than the origami that you're doing now.*
MM: *It helps me think.*

This issue of McNeill's thinking patterns came into question at the beginning of the trial when Alford unsuccessfully argued that McNeill was unfit to stand for trial.

Psychological Evaluation

McNeill was tested by four separate physicians to determine his competency to stand trial. Dr. James Hilkey, the main physician, evaluated McNeill over five sessions that totaled sixteen hours. One of McNeill's psychological "tells" was his penchant for closing his eyes, pretending to be asleep. In his original police interview, his interrogator became irritated with McNeill for exhibiting sleep-like behavior. "Show some respect and open your eyes. Sit up! Sit up in your chair!" the agent yelled. When Dr. Hilkey questioned McNeill about what he described as a "waxy posture, rigid with his eyes closed," McNeill explained that he closed his eyes to cut off his sense of sight, which he believed would enhance his other senses.

McNeill believed he had special powers from a young age, offering as evidence his ability to predict events or determine the sex of a child before birth. McNeill believed in a god called "Sophia" who manifested through the wisdom in his mind.

McNeill further believed that he held an electromagnetic connection to three jury members and this connection would be helpful to him throughout the trial. Despite these alarming revelations, the doctor found him competent to stand trial, adding that, "If anything, there was a tendency for McNeill to minimize or to deny psychological problems," a phenomenon he called *faking good*. McNeill disagreed with the doctor's findings, accusing Hilkey of "telepathically altering his mental evaluation." McNeill's jury of eight men and four women may not have sensed his magnetic connection, but they did sense his guilt and they sensed it unanimously.

Sentencing

McNeill's guilty verdict was not unexpected. It took the public three seconds of watching the video surveillance and the jury seven and one half hours to find him so. The only tension remaining in the whole affair was his punishment. Would the jury recommend life in prison without parole or the death sentence? McNeill arrived at court in a short-sleeve, green polo shirt, which was several sizes too large for him. He wrapped his long dreadlocks up into a French twist. His over-sized shirt, coupled with the enormous twist of his long dreadlocks, gave the back of his body a cartoonish look, and somehow the exaggerated clothing and wild bouffant hair made the rest of him look small.

JA: *Will the defendant please stand.*

McNeill stood and shrugged his shoulders as if to stretch. He put his hands behind him to pull down his shirt. For the first time during his trial, he looked uncertain.

Suddenly, the long years between the crime and the trial, the acute pain stirred up by the testimony and expert witnesses regarding Shaniya's final hours, the slow, sluggish pace of justice quickened its tempo and in an excited and nervous rush, his sentence was blurted out by the woman appointed as jury foreman (JF):

JF: *As to the issues and recommendations as to punishment as to the defendant Mario McNeill in file number 09CRS66040 as to issue number one: yes, as to issue number two: yes, as to issue number three: yes, as to issue number four: yes. The jury has returned as to the recommendation as to the defendant Mario McNeill that he be sentenced to death.*

The entirety and sum of McNeill's thirty-three years alive came down to a forty-two-second monologue spoken by a young girl in the language of the law. It is impossible to know how many words Shaniya was afforded before she died, but these sixty-three words pronounced a legal sentence that would end McNeill's life.

During her statement, McNeill gave a slight, almost unnoticeable, gentle nod of yes.

JA: *Is this the unanimous recommendation of the jury?*

JF: *Yes.*

JA: *So say you all by raising your hand. The court sees twelve hands. Thank you. Have a seat. The defense may have a seat.*

Everyone sat in silence and waited to see McNeill leave the courtroom. But Judge Ammons had to perform a legal commission before McNeill was cuffed and ejected. The judge then addressed McNeill.

JA: *The prisoner, Mario Andretti McNeill, having been found guilty of murder in the first degree is therefore ordered and adjudged that the same Mario Andretti McNeill be, and he is, hereby sentenced to death* [pause] *and the sheriff of Cumberland County, North Carolina, in whose custody the defendant now is, shall forthwith deliver the said prisoner Mario Andretti McNeill to the warden of the state penitentiary at Raleigh, North Carolina, and the warden shall cause the said prisoner Mario Andretti*

McNeill to be put to death as thou provided. May God have mercy on your soul.

The court officials busied themselves with paperwork and filing while the gallery and McNeill sat quietly waiting for instructions. The judge soon addressed the court.

JA: *All right. Stand up, Mr. McNeill. You did not have to kill that child.*

MM: *I didn't.*

JA: *Get him out of here now.*

McNeill put his hands behind his back, waiting for the cuffs, but the bailiffs, intent on pleasing the judge who appeared quite sour and agitated by the proceedings, started to walk him to the door without cuffs in order to "get him out of here now." McNeill took advantage of this tiny bit of freedom by walking past the judge and saying, "You know I didn't." The judge looked at the bailiffs who immediately stopped McNeill and cuffed him before leading him through the door that would be his first doorway of many toward his journey to his death chamber.

Antoinette Davis

Antoinette Davis' defense team, D.W. Bray and his wife, Dollie, set their intention and focus on two objectives: they wanted Judge Ammons to dismiss the charges based on a Miranda violation and failing that, they wanted Ammons to suppress Davis' confession tape given during her police interrogation. Without this tape, the prosecution had no case. There was no other evidence against Davis. There were no phone records, no history with McNeill and no forensic evidence pointing to Davis having any hand in the death of her daughter. Even McNeill, who said very little at all, told police multiple times that he did not know Antoinette and that she did not buy drugs from him. The only evidence against Davis was Davis herself, and if her attorney could get the confession thrown out, Davis would walk free. Bray presented both of these legal strategies in pre-trial motions on the morning of Friday, October 18, 2013. Ammons had sentenced McNeill to death just four months earlier.

First, Bray argued to have the charges vacated based on a Miranda violation of her Fifth Amendment right. For four days after Davis' 911 call to report Shaniya missing, the police drove to her Aunt Lorraine's house where Davis was staying since the trailer had been condemned. Every morning, Davis dutifully climbed into the police car and allowed herself to be taken to the police station down on Hay Street. She spent those days in an exhausted state of confusion and fear. Antoinette told me, "They kept telling me that I knew where she was at."

Bray argued that Davis was not properly mirandized during these police "conversations" and that she didn't fully understand that she was not under arrest. Antoinette confirmed this for me during one of our phone conversations. She said, "They made me think I was under arrest. I asked them could I go to the bathroom and they made me go with a female officer. She came into the bathroom with me." The prosecutors responded that Davis willingly came to the police department and was free to leave when she wished. They stated that Davis was not under arrest at the time of the interrogation and therefore did not require a reading of her Miranda rights.

This is a common deception used by law enforcement when attempting to elicit a confession. The Fayetteville Police Department behaved in a manner consistent with an arrest by transporting Davis in a police car, holding her in an interrogation room, taking her cell phone and not allowing her bathroom or smoking privileges without an officer present. But they did not officially arrest her and therefore were not legally required to mirandize her. The judge ruled against Bray's request for a dismissal of the charges.

This left Bray with one legal maneuver in an attempt to avoid a trial—and avoiding trial was the Brays' unwavering goal. Dollie Bray told me that Antoinette "would have been lynched outside of the courthouse" if the public had their way. She insisted Antoinette "could never get a fair trial in this town or any town." She pointed to the *Nancy Grace* coverage that "blew this thing up to a national level." She told me with veiled pride, "Oprah's people were trying to get me to talk to them." But Oprah's people were no match for Dollie Bray; she would never give up information about Antoinette. For all her bluster and fast, intelligent loud-mouthing, Bray remained protective of Antoinette. She would not sell out to Oprah. But all of this loyalty meant very little inside a courtroom. D.W. Bray had lost his motion to vacate the charges; he needed the police confession tape suppressed if his client was going to have a chance at freedom.

But dismissing the confession was no small matter. Despite The Innocence Project's study that one out of four people wrongfully convicted but later exonerated by DNA made false confessions to the police during interrogation, confessions are still heavily relied upon during trial. Jurors have a difficult time overcoming a confession. Why would someone confess to a crime that she did not commit? Studies have shown that there are key contributing factors related to false confessions; among them are diminished capacity due to exhaustion, ignorance of the law, coercion and a misunderstanding of the situation. These were the very issues the Brays intended to bring before Judge Ammons. According to court testimony at the pre-trial motions, the Brays presented a strong case for Antoinette's exhaustion and ignorance of the law. They pointed out that she had no criminal record, not even a traffic violation, and had never seen the inside of a police station. She had no experience with police arrests or procedures.

At the time she was questioned, she had been terrified because her daughter was still missing and she was held in an interrogation room, not certain she was allowed to leave. This questioning went on for four of the six days Shaniya remained missing. She said they kept "pushing her to tell them about Clarence Coe." Later, after the video surveillance tape was released, they pressed her just as hard to give up information relating to McNeill. Initially, the police speculated that a second man was involved, and although this theory was short-lived, Antoinette was again pushed to give them information about this second man. She knew nothing of any man but with their promises of "tell us what we want to know and you can go home," she took a gamble on their honesty. Antoinette's trust and efforts to appease the police became her undoing. She finally gave them a story they accepted about a $200 debt but certainly never added that she sold her daughter. She told me that amount was in her head based on Brenda's required deposit for the trailer. Antoinette was shocked when she was told to stand and place her hands behind her back. Now she was officially under arrest.

Bray (DWB) argued that the police bullied his client who was already under duress from her current pregnancy. Furthermore, Davis was confused and almost numb with Shaniya's disappearance. Additionally, DSS had taken custody of her son Carlesio the day Shaniya was kidnapped.

DWB: *She was arguably coerced and bullied by two enforcement officers. By the fourth day of questioning, court records indicate that "she was sobbing."*

Antoinette admits to being confused and scared. Her daughter was missing and even if she did hold information concerning *who* her daughter might have been with, she had no understanding or knowledge of *where* she was or *why* she was gone. But the police kept at her—four days of interrogations with each day holding six hours of questioning, yelling and judging.

At first, Antoinette offered the police her boyfriend, Clarence Coe, as a suspect. She said the police "already had him in their sights and so I just gave them what they wanted." Davis told police that Coe had "punched her [Shaniya] in the cheek and she fell to the ground." She told them that he scooped up Shaniya and she never saw either of them again. Coe was arrested February 11, one day after Shaniya was kidnapped. But, a day later, the surveillance footage of McNeill holding the child betrayed her "confession." Coe was released while McNeill voluntarily surrendered. The police went back after Davis, saying, "You know what happened; tell us about McNeill." Antoinette told them she didn't know McNeill beyond his role as her sister's drug dealer. The prosecutors admitted that by the fourth day of her interrogation, she "broke." But was "broke" defined as finally revealing the real truth?

Or was it defined as agreeing to the interpretation the interrogators wanted?

According to the tape-recorded interview, it was at this point that Davis (AD) confessed to selling Shaniya for $200.

> AD: [Weeping] *I gave her to him to cover $200. He was only supposed to have sex.*

If her confession was coerced, I never understood how she came up with such a damning and detailed story. I asked her about it at one of our prison visitations. She told me they were pressuring her about McNeill. I asked her if one of the police officers "guided" her confession. "Where did you come up with the idea of selling Shaniya?" I asked her.

She looked right into me. "I don't know where it came from."

I pushed. "But it must have been one of the police officers suggesting it. Did they put the idea into your head?"

She looked at me for just a second before saying, "No, I don't know why I said it. It just came to me. I don't know why I said it." It was in a later conversation she told me that Brenda needed $200 dollars as a deposit to get into the Sleepy Hollow trailer. She didn't know if that was in her mind that day or not.

Prosecuting attorney Billy West felt he knew where the idea came from. He believed that McNeill lent Davis $200 to buy food and pay for a hotel room when she and her children were homeless. He told WRAL in an interview that the information in an autopsy report that claimed the debt to be drug-related was incorrect.

West believed that McNeill went to Sleepy Hollow that night of November 9, 2009, to have sex with Antoinette's neighbor, Tanisia. That's what Tanisia testified to during McNeill's trial. West speculated that when Tanisia had fallen asleep and didn't answer her door, McNeill went to Brenda Davis' home and demanded that she either pay him the $200 or have sex with him. Police believed that Antoinette Davis refused him and that McNeill took Shaniya instead. West said that in part of her confession, Davis claimed to have attempted to stop McNeill from taking Shaniya. For reasons that West never explained, the police chose not to believe that part of Davis' "confession." West did admit that there was no evidence of a drug debt or sale of the child.

Bray argued for all of the tapes to be thrown out but Ammons ruled against him. This was the double negative the Brays had been dreading. It was at this ruling, mid-morning on Friday, October 18, that Antoinette's life changed.

She told me that her understanding was that her attorneys had to meet with the judge that Friday morning but that her trial would start that afternoon. She didn't understand that their morning meeting would determine their course of action through the rest of that day, which would then affect the course of Antoinette's life forever.

Once the Brays lost their pre-trial motions they set their sights on a plea deal. Dollie was acutely defensive about this deal when we spoke in person. "Antoinette was facing three life sentences. I didn't take my counsel lightly. How could I send her to trial facing three life sentences?" She asked me this without actually wanting an answer.

Antoinette remembers sitting in a room inside the courthouse that morning while her attorney had his meeting. Antoinette said she was in there all morning, thinking she was waiting for trial. It was quiet and boring as she sat, in her tan, short-sleeve prison uniform, waiting for the Brays to return from court. Suddenly the room was full of people and noise. She said there were "lawyers everywhere" and they were talking around her, to each other. She said that this noise and paper shuffling and energy went on for some time when Dollie approached her, telling her that they had lost their pre-trial motions. Antoinette did not know what this meant but soon learned when Dollie advised her to take a plea deal.

"I didn't know what she was saying. She was crying and said that I wouldn't have a chance in court, that I should just say I did it." Antoinette recalls everything moving very quickly as she was escorted to the courtroom. And then everything was quiet again.

Antoinette Davis stood before Judge Ammons as her nine charges were read in a very still courtroom:

> second-degree murder
> human trafficking
> felony child abuse with prostitution
> conspiracy to commit sex abuse of a child by an adult offender
> first-degree kidnapping
> sexual servitude
> felony child abuse involving a sex act
> taking indecent liberties with a child

She heard herself say *guilty* as she entered nine Alford Pleas. This plea meant that she was not admitting guilt but rather acknowledging that if she were to face a jury, the prosecution could present enough evidence to convict her. This was, of course, inherently incorrect. The prosecution had nothing against Davis but her confusing and at times, contradictory confession tape. The Alford Plea was treated as a *guilty* plea and sentencing guidelines were according to a *guilty* plea. After the formal sentencing, Antoinette was permitted to address the court and gallery which included Shaniya's father, Brad Lockhart.

> AD: *I wanted my baby back; I wanted my baby with me; I wanted my baby with her brother. I didn't . . . you know . . . I didn't really think too much about her surroundings, which I should have. I admit I was wrong about that. I never said I was a perfect mother, but I was a good mother. I did what I had to do to provide for them. I did what I had to do to make sure they were all right because I didn't have any help from anybody.*

At this point Antoinette addressed Brad Lockhart, saying she was sorry. She spoke to the judge and did not look at Lockhart.

> AD: *I'm sorry. I should have never taken Shaniya away from him and his family. I want to say I did what I could as a mother. I was there to protect my daughter. He knew that. And I knew he felt the same way himself.*

The judge allowed Lockhart (BL) to make a statement in response. And so the man who had hired Antoinette to strip and have sex with him, which eventually produced the child at the center of proceedings spoke directly to her.

> BL: *I forgave you a long time ago, and I'm sure Shaniya did too. If you dig deeply, you might help others by telling your story.*

Judge Ammons ordered Davis to stand. He did not share Lockhart's magnanimity.

> JA: *I saw you on that videotape. "All he was supposed to do was have sex with her. That's it. That's all.*

That's it." You could have saved your daughter's life, but you did not. You had the opportunity and the means to save Shaniya's life, and you did not. You are not a good mother. This did not have to happen. Take her away, please.

    This court proceeding does not settle the questions that linger and float around in my mind. There are times when I believe Antoinette is guilty of something, but I never can definitively pin down any crime with precision. Guilty of birthing too many children? Me too. Guilty of living a life of poverty and lack? Check. Guilty of choosing men incapable or unwilling to support the children they produced? Again, me too. Antoinette stood guilty, like me, of being poor and pregnant. The public saw her as getting away with something that they had to pay for.

    My lifestyle in the church was so similar to her lifestyle in her neighborhood in that we shared the nouns: fear, lack, worthlessness and despair. But her nouns were wrapped around adjectives including, black, female, welfare and trailer park, and these modifiers created a picture of entitlement. And so the public, furious over her lazy, public-assistance check cashing, found her guilty before there was even a crime to attribute to her. The false report of what would become her defining crime was written and published long before Antoinette's day in court. To the public, Antoinette was guilty even before Shaniya was taken.

    Certainly, even the prosecutor admits that she was not guilty of selling Shaniya for drug money. And yet this was the crime that captured the media and the nation. The original source of this rumor was rooted to a "faulty statement on the coroner's report." No public official has taken ownership of the statement, nor is there any narrative to support how the statement ended up on a public document. But the whys and the whens mean very little when looking at the whos. Antoinette was a poor, uneducated black woman living in a filthy trailer. These facts produce a picture that satisfies the public's perception of welfare mom. Although Antoinette had no drugs in her system that night, the public sees her as a lazy, habitually pregnant, crack-smoking "welfare ho," as she was called in the press. And it was this fiction that created the outrage against her. Never mind that she didn't buy or use drugs, she had worked as stripper, had three children by three different fathers and lived on the bad side of Fayetteville. Once the faulty coroner's report was released, the public, already frothing at the blood in the water spilled by McNeill—a drug-pushing, dreadlock-wearing black man with a smirk—pounced on Antoinette who came to represent all they loathed about poverty and black women. Antoinette was never presented as a person but rather a representation of a prejudice pervasive in public opinion. Strangely, had the media slowed down, had the public demanded evidence or even an intelligent conversation, they could have satisfied their anger against welfare moms by pointing their privileged fingers at other players in the trailer. But the police set their gaze upon Shaniya's mother and their gaze remained focused and unwavering until Antoinette was publicly shackled and properly punished for the crimes that labeled her. These crimes hung upon her by the time she ended her 911 call to the police.

> *Now begin in the middle, and later learn the beginning; the end will take care of itself.*
> – Harlan Ellison, "'Repent Harlequin!' Said the Ticktockman"

Red Chair, Yellow Chair

I PULLED INTO the prisonyard full of fear. I was afraid of everything: that I would have to be stripped searched to get in, that I would have to use the bathroom while there, that I would forget everything we spoke about, but mostly that Antoinette would not like me. My husband walked me to the gate where I stood with an older-looking couple holding a 2-year-old little girl. It was hot outside, even at nine in the morning, and the little girl was sweating from running around the little yard like a chicken. Another man, thin and tired-looking, walked up with us and joined the couple in what looked like an informal line. I was nervous that my skirt was too short despite my actually measuring the distance between my knee and hemline. I wanted to take in some breath mints but couldn't risk them being found and then being turned away. I had read over the list of rules for visitation and had them mostly memorized. I was terrified of being rejected and terrified of being allowed in. I felt this terror in equal measure.

I asked Simeon to take my picture, standing by a large tree outside the gatehouse. I felt self-conscious standing there smiling in front of a prison. All those people in line—it had grown to about twelve people—watched me pose. Simeon, who has a bad reputation for taking a very long time to snap the picture, seemed unaware of my distress from the audience. Just as he was about to take the picture, an armed guard called from a vehicle sitting nearby, "No cameras on prison property. Put that back in your car."

My throat went dry, and now I worried that I would be on the inside before Simeon got back to me from the long walk to the car. He lacked my concerns. "It will be all right, Abigail. I'll be back before you go in, I promise." He turned and walked in his confident way, and I started to believe him. It was going to be all right.

I wandered over to join the others. There was a small cluster of people on the sidewalk now. A woman near the front of our sad gathering told a man farther back in the line to take off his hat. "They won't let you in with it on," she said simply. He removed his hat, and some of us gave a fake laugh in an attempt to relieve the tension. Nobody asked who was visiting whom, which would have led to the real question on all of our minds which was, *What did your person do to get in here?* If it had been a contest, I know I would have won with such salacious felonies as *murder* and *prostitution of a child*. After the hat woman opened it up, a few others joined in small talk as we waited on the sidewalk in the bright morning sun.

"Sure is hot today," someone said.

"Yup," came a reply.

The older woman at the front, who had become our matriarch, pushed the boundaries a bit. "You know they got no air-conditioning in there." She nodded her head toward the massive chain-link fence with the barbed wire rolled around the top.

I remembered Antoinette's trailer at Sleepy Hollow in Fayetteville and wondered which location was worse. Of course it would be prison, but it would be difficult to argue against the idea Sleepy Hollow didn't represent a very different sort of prison. Antoinette told me once that she "hated the person I was before I came in here." At Sleepy Hollow, she lived in the middle of affluence and opportunity and yet she remained trapped and poor. In prison, she lived in the middle of prisoners, some affluent, some not. But prison, unlike Sleepy Hollow, is an equalizer. She joined a population stripped of social markers. She could explore facets of herself that would be impossible to explore within the trailer at Sleepy Hollow. Prison is awful, of course. It is meant to be. But it is possible that in there, Antoinette found a tiny fragment of freedom that would not have otherwise been available to her.

The guard opened the secured door to the gatehouse and motioned for the first couple to come forward just as Simeon walked back up and joined me in line. He wouldn't be permitted inside. The process to visit an inmate is long and protracted, involving forms mailed from "the offender" to the potential visitor with the potential visitor manually filling out all the blocks and sending in copies of every official identification card afforded to one person. All the information is collected and scanned and reviewed. One day a letter of acceptance arrives, telling the potential visitor that she has been found worthy to visit their state property, and by this, they do not mean their prison; they mean their prisoner. It is a small kind of accomplishment to be officially found a low risk within a prison bureaucracy.

I moved up the concrete sidewalk, inching closer to the gatehouse door, and blocked the sun with my arms. I could see some prisoners on the other side of the fence. They wore tan colored dresses or slacks and looked back at our line with equal interest. I watched them closely, trying to absorb "prison habitat" but ended up feeling like Jane Goodall watching the primates and turned my eyes away ashamed. It was finally my turn to enter the gatehouse, and when the guard motioned for me to move forward, I panicked. I turned to Simeon who hugged me and pushed me forward at the same time. I walked toward the guard in a stupor of fear and dread. What if I got trapped in there? What if an inmate or guard threatened me? One step, two steps, three steps, breathe.

Escorted into a tiny room, I was asked for my identification cards and the offender's number attached to my visit. I never got used to that term *offender,* finding it, among other things, offensive, but it was the word used on all of the forms and, now that I was here, by all the guards. I signed in on a print-out list attached to a clipboard and wrote Antoinette's offender number, 1177095, in the little box next to my name.

I tutor in a Writing Center at a small college in Asheville. After each session with a student, I fill out a form to track the visit to update the instructor with the details. It's a simple form, requiring me to ask the students a series of questions to fill in the boxes. The first section on the form asks for the student's identification number. It is a seven-digit number assigned to them at their acceptance into the college. It feels demoralizing, somehow, to ask for those numbers before I ask for their names. They always comply; not one student in all these years has made a fuss about being signified as a number rather than a name, but it feels backwards to me.

Since I began this project, I think of Antoinette each time I type the student's seven-digit number, considering the colossal difference between her signifier and the student's. Seven digits, simple numbers with equal value, when issued into a human's personal story, convey a meaning that can represent hope or despair.

I waited for one of the guards—there were four of them inside the small gatehouse—to match all my information and clear me for entry. I was then asked to walk through a scanner. I was relieved beyond measure to find that I was not told to disrobe before walking through but worried that other visitors might slip in a shiv or a shank. I consistently confuse the verb from the noun. Does one shiv with a shank or is it the other way around? Regardless of the grammar, I was scared of both.

After I passed the scan test, I was told to put out my right hand. A guard pressed a rubber stamp into some ink and then pushed it into my hand. I was reminded of my younger years when I went clubbing and used the smeared black ink on the back of my hand as a badge of honor the next day in class. But when I pulled my hand away, there was no mark. "I don't think it took," I said.

The guard paid no attention and responded with "Face the door and wait for the click. Do not attempt to open the door."

This was the back door to the building, and so I moved to the door and stood with my arms at my sides, feeling powerless and irrationally upset that I was not allowed to open my own door. *I'm not the prisoner here*, I thought to myself, but when I would come back through this door I would question that assumption. The door clicked and magically, like the Cheshire Cat, a female guard appeared on the other side and opened it for me.

She gestured toward a building that was ten feet away, and I started walking there. She kept pace at my heels. I approached the door to the building, and she gave the same rote instructions. I stood with my arms at my side and at the click, yet another guard opened the door that I entered. I was officially on the inside. The building looked a lot like the Fellowship Hall at my childhood Perry Christian Church. It had those same cinder-block walls and brown, square-tiled floor. There was a bathroom along the back wall. My alarm increased to a full Dick Cheney code orange as I saw the sign posted "Out of Order" on the women's door. Immediately, I had to pee.

The guard gestured for me to walk in front of her, which is an uncertain position, considering I did not know where we were going. But I am dutiful, and it was then that I noticed the plastic chairs all lined up like soldiers against the wall. They were yellow and their happy disposition looked out of place here against the drab grey walls and weathered brown floor. About two inches from the row of yellow chairs sat an identical row of red chairs. They faced each other. I understood that offenders would sit in the yellow chairs with their backs against the wall and the visitors would sit in front of them, occupying the red ones. This was really happening.

The guard pointed to a red chair one down from that older couple who had come in before me. I caught the guard's eye and tried to convey my eagerness to obey. I sat down and faced forward with my arms hanging down at my sides to show her that I intended to conform. In that short walk from the gatehouse to the visiting room, I had become a sycophant.

I heard them call "Antoinette Davis to the Visiting Hall" over the loudspeaker that broadcast throughout the entire prison, reminding me of the "Incoming Wounded" announcement on *MASH*. I tried to picture her in her cell. Was she fixing her hair, was she as nervous as I was? There was a mild commotion near a door to my right where I saw a prisoner enter, escorted by a guard. It was not Antoinette. This girl looked like a high school senior with her long, black hair pulled into a neat ponytail that bounced with each step. She walked through a door into a shower-room-looking space where she was strip searched behind a curtain. At the end of the visit, the prisoners are required to reverse this procedure, stripping again in case a visitor—within the view of seven rotating guards who walked up and down the aisles between the chair sets the entire time we visited (one hour and forty-two minutes)—is able to transfer contraband.

I've watched *Orange is the New Black* and understand that people are unfathomably clever when it comes to transferring and storing prison contraband, but I couldn't imagine anyone smart enough to receive even something as small as a cigarette under the watchful and ever-present marching of the guards, much less secure said contraband on their person with such intimacy that it would require a strip search to find it. The young, fresh-faced-looking girl came back through the door from the shower area and was escorted to the couple sitting near me with the 2-year-old. They stood up and hugged her while the guard looked on, and then, after the short hug, the guard pointed to the yellow chair and the girl took her seat. She grabbed hands with the couple, whom I assumed were her parents (making the 2-year-old her child?), and did not let go the entire visit.

The visits were supposed to be for two hours, but every time I visited, I could only count on an hour and forty minutes. It just took so long to get the visitors through the gatehouse and the prisoner to the visiting hall that the visit time became truncated. Additionally, depending on the mood of the guards, we might be asked to leave up to twenty minutes early. The guards would just make the announcement to the room, "Visiting hours are over," at which we would make small movements of protest, pointing to watches or glancing at the big clock on the wall. After a muffled collective groan, we would all stand up, arms to our sides and wait for permission to hug our offender and then line up to leave the hall. The prisoners were required to sit in their yellow seats until all visitors were cleared and then they would undergo their second strip search within two hours and finally be released back into their prison routine.

The visitors were escorted back through the gatehouse where we were required to hold our hand under a green light. There, an image appeared that changed every visit. It would be close to impossible for an offender and visitor to switch places with this secret invisible stamp. I thought of ways it could happen but was always left with the image of an escaped prisoner driving away and the visitor trapped in an unjustified jail cell thinking, *What did I just do?*

When Antoinette came through that first door, I did not recognize her. As many times as I had seen her face in the videos and newsprint, she did not look as I had expected. Because her voice is so soft and her manner softer still, I expected a small, diminutive woman. So when an Amazon woman of over six feet stood in the doorway with a much shorter guard, I was thrown off. She looked over at me—I had sent a picture a few weeks earlier—and we caught eyes in that awkward blind date kind of way. We both looked away but looked back immediately to size the other person up. She was just so tall. As she was escorted back to the shower room area, I noticed that she was the only prisoner so far to wear blue jeans. Actually, blue jeans is a misnomer. They were made from a dyed polyester blend and were held up with an elastic waist. The jeans sort of hurt my feelings as I glanced around the room and saw that every single prisoner sitting in a yellow chair was wearing the prison-issued tan dress. The dress tried, and successfully accomplished its task, to be drab and shapeless, but it did sport two jaunty pockets on the front. The 2-year-old next to me kept sticking her hands in her mom's (?) pockets and coming up empty for treasures. I imagined this ponytailed girl sitting alone in her cell after the visit, placing her hand over the invisible prints the little girl had left on the dress. A phantom connection known only to the mother.

By now Antoinette had been escorted to her chair opposite me. I stood up awkwardly and leaned in for a hug. My head landed on her chest, and I pulled away, self-conscious and embarrassed. She sat down and her granddaddy long legs smashed up against mine in the small space they allotted between the chairs. We would bang and bump up against each other through much of our visit. As I tended to do in our phone conversations, I talked at lightning speed and covered dozens of subjects that held no true import to our being together in this space in such a manner.

We stole glances at each other's bodies and clothing during this initial burst and spurt of conversation. She had a butterfly tattoo on her arm and told me it represented a rebirth or chance for a new life. We spoke of the cheap material of the prison uniforms and discussed the privatization of prisons and how it will affect the population now that it has become capitalized. At one point she crossed those long legs, and a guard made a small noise and pointed. Antoinette immediately uncrossed her legs. "What was all that about?" I asked, as I uncrossed my own legs in order to achieve my mission of invisibility while on the "inside."

She laughed, as she had through most of our visit. "Well, I guess you're not allowed to cross your legs," she said. "It's probably so you can't hide contraband," she added, reminding me that this was her first visit as well. She was also learning the rules. In the five years she had been incarcerated, she had received zero visitors. Not even Dollie Bray.

She assured me that this crossing-legs rule did not apply to me, but I wasn't willing to take any chances. She said that I could stand up to use the restroom (had it not been out of service) but that prisoners were not allowed out of their yellow chairs until the room was cleared. She informed me that if she stood up at any time during our scheduled visit, the session would be over, and she would be immediately escorted back to a holding area until I was escorted back to the gatehouse.

I told her this was a good thing, giving her some authority over the visit. "What if an abusive boyfriend managed to get on your list and came in here to badger you?"

She laughed and said she would never get a boyfriend, even the badgering kind.

"Well, maybe so, but at least you wouldn't have to sit here for two hours and take it. You could stand up and the guards would protect you by removing you from an uncomfortable situation."

She rebuked my idea. "The guards aren't going to protect me. They don't care a thing about me." She told me she just keeps her head down and tries to stay out of notice. I knew the feeling.

"Antoinette," I openly asked, "how could this happen?" I gestured to the prison.

She looked around the room at the guards and the bars and then back to me.

"Did you sell Shaniya to McNeill?"

She spoke in her low, soft voice, "No."

* * *

The visit was memorable only due to the occasion and setting. I was knocking knees with the fabled and infamous Antoinette Davis. We were sitting inside a close custody security prison with security cameras, high voltage fencing and guards surrounding us. I sat inches away from a convicted felon. Had she gone to trial and lost instead of taking a plea, she could have been sentenced up to three life terms. But sitting there in my red chair, I found nothing distinguishing about her. While she held unique physical markers—those huge, brown eyes and her mouth that smiles from its resting position, her elegant stature and her enormous feet—had she not been in that uniform, in that setting, in that chair, she would have been unremarkable.

She laughed about funny things, she expressed pain when glancing at the 2-year-old who grew restless beside us, she showed deference and respect to the guard, all of which, when summed up, made her normal. We could have just as easily switched places and nothing would be different. Nothing marked her as monster and me as saint except for the color of our chairs. Had one thing been different in our lives, one turn right instead of left, either one of us could have been sitting in the other color.

I had some privilege on my side, but had one or two things shifted in my life, I could just as easily be sitting in the yellow chair that day. And these shifts weren't dramatic. Out of context they were tiny things, but the results had favored me. If I pulled myself out of my circumstances and put myself in Antoinette's life, I believe I would have made similar choices. If I had lived as myself within Antoinette's life, I would be in prison as well. I know for a certainty I would have chosen a plea deal over truth, out of fear. I do not believe I could have improved upon her situation.

Indeed, based on small gusts of luck, I barely escaped the yellow chair living my own life. My place in that red chair was almost arbitrary. Had Antoinette and I switched places that day, we could both have justified the exchange. I was no more worthy of the red chair than she was of the yellow.

Our relationship is an odd one. We were both drawn to each other because she was a person with a story, and I was a person who could tell it. We traveled many of the same metaphorical miles to arrive at our chairs, but for chance or privilege or fate, she ended up in the yellow chair and I was escorted to the red one. When it was time to go (twelve minutes early), we hugged. I held on for an extra second, wanting to press my care and devotion into her. The visitors lined up with arms at our sides without a second thought; the inculcation of the prison system was that thorough. As we waited our turn to be escorted out, the prisoners watched each other and us as we watched ourselves and them. In my final glimpse of Antoinette, sitting there in the chair like a gazelle on a hillside, I recognized a trait I lacked in myself. I saw dignity.

Antoinette will spend the next seventeen to twenty-one years of her life within the Raleigh Correctional Institute for Women. She walked into that prison because of events that both happened to her and events that she caused. I walked out of that prison because of events that both happened to me and events that I caused. I felt a fragility in the difference.

APPENDIX

Appendix A: McNeill's Letter from Prison

> MAILED FROM CCDC
>
> Press,
>
> I did not take or kidnap Shaniya Davis, I did not purchase, buy, trade, sell or exchange Shaniya Davis, I did not molest, sexually assault, rape or ravish Shaniya Davis, I did not kill, murder, or take Shaniya Davis's life, nor did I have any prior or before hand knowledge as to what was to and/or did occur.
>
> Mario McNeill
> Mario McNeill

Letter credit:
http://fayobserver.com/fayobserver.com/files/f6/f66e5ffb-7e6e-411e-abe6-33c7f2b12abe.pdf

Appendix B: Davis' 911 Transcript

911: *911 what is your emergency?*

CALLER: *Yes, ma'am. My name is Antoinette Davis at 1116A Sleepy Hollow.*

911: *Ma'am.*

CALLER: *My name is Antoinette Davis at 1116A Sleep Hollow.*

911: *Okay, I'm not getting your address clearly; can you slow down a little bit and tell me again?*

CALLER: *1116A Sleepy Hollow.*

911: *115A?*

CALLER: *16.*

911: *One six?*

CALLER: *Yes, ma'am.*

911: *Okay, okay, ma'am, how can I help you?*

CALLER: *I woke up this morning and my daughter was not in the house. I don't know if she walked out, or I don't know what's going on, but she's not here.*

911: *How old is your daughter?*

CALLER: *She is five.*

911: *Five?*

CALLER: *Yes, ma'am.*

911: *Okay, what time did you wake up? When did you last see her?*

CALLER: *I saw her, uh, at five-thirty last night.*

911: *5:30 last night? Is that when you put her to bed?*

CALLER: *Yes, ma'am. No, when she went back to bed.*

911: *[typing] Okay. That was five this morning, is that what you're telling me?*

CALLER: *Yes, ma'am.*

911: *Okay, um, were there any doors open or anything like that?*
CALLER: *She know how to unlock the front door.*
911: *Okay. Okay. [typing] What is her name?*
CALLER: *Shaniya Davis.*
911: *Spell that name for me.*
CALLER: *S H A N I Y A.*
911: *[typing] And is she white, black or Hispanic?*
CALLER: *She's mixed.*
911: *Okay.*
CALLER: *She's biracial.*
911: *And what was she wearing?*
CALLER: *She's wearing just a blue, big old blue shirt with designs on the front but her hair is out.*
911: *Okay. Does she have on, um, any pants?*
CALLER: *She didn't take no shoes, no pants, no nothing.*
911: *Did she have on underwear?*
CALLER: *Yes, ma'am.*
911: *Okay. What—do you know what color?*
CALLER: *They're white and they got pink, I guess, I can't—I can't really remember. They are like white with pink designs on them.*
911: *Okay, okay, and you said none of the doors were open?*
CALLER: *No, ma'am, they were locked, but she's knows how to unlock the front door.*
911: *Was it closed?*
CALLER: *Yes, ma'am.*
911: *This morning? And you said it was around five-thirty?*
CALLER: *Yes, ma'am.*
911: *Okay. [typing] Have you checked the neighborhood?*
CALLER: *I checked everywhere. I haven't checked the back end of the neighborhood yet, but I checked the front end.*

I'm just, I don't know what else to do. I'm so—I'm—I don't know what else to do.
911: *Are there anymore, um, juveniles inside the home?*
CALLER: *There's my son, but he's here!*
911: *Okay. And your door was not unlocked, that's what you're telling me?*
CALLER: *No, it was not unlocked. But I'm telling you she knows how to unlock it. I'm hoping that she didn't unlock it and walk out.*
911: *Okay. What's the number you're calling me from, ma'am?*
CALLER: *[blocked]*
911: *Okay, we already got your call in and are going to get someone out. You said her hair was out?*
CALLER: *Yes, it's like a bushy Afro.*
911: *How much does she weigh, do you know?*
CALLER: *I don't know, ma'am. I don't remember.*
911: *Okay. All right, ma'am, um, just try to, you know, check your home again and check around the neighborhood. If anything changes, call us back. But we already got the call in, and we're going to get someone out as soon as we can, okay?*
CALLER: *All right.*
911: *All right, ma'am. Thank you.*

photo credit: The Shaniya Davis Memorial Page: www.findagrave.com

JUNE 14, 2004 –
NOVEMBER 10, 2009

www.ingramcontent.com/pod-product-compliance
Lightning Source LLC
Chambersburg PA
CBHW051646040426
42446CB00009B/1004